Phonographics

PHONOGRAPHICS
CONTEMPORARY ALBUM COVER ART & DESIGN
BY BRAD BENEDICT & LINDA BARTON

COLLIER BOOKS
A Division of Macmillan Publishing Co., Inc.
New York

TO OUR PARENTS

Macmillan Publishing Co., Inc.
866 Third Avenue, New York, N.Y. 10022
Collier Macmillan Canada, Ltd.
First Collier Books Edition 1977
Design: Rod Dyer   .
Library of Congress Catalog Card Number: 77-82314
Phonographics is also published in a hardcover edition by
Macmillan Publishing Co., Inc.
Printed in the United States of America

We wish to extend a very special Thank You to the following friends whose talent, help and experience have made this project a reality: Dave Willardson, Rod Dyer, Rick Seireeni, John Hartnett, Amanda Vaill, Beth Rashbaum, Rusty Gutwillig, Charlie Perry and Peter Plagens.

We would like to express our gratitude to the many creative art directors within the music industry whose cooperation has been invaluable: John Berg, Columbia Records; John Cabalka, Warner Bros. Records; Phil Carroll, Fantasy Records; Bob Defrin, Atlantic Records; Jules Halfant, Vanguard Records; Diana Kaylan, Capricorn Records; Lucy Kleps, London Records; Roy Kohara, Capitol Records; Jim Ladwig, AGI/Chicago; Acy Lehman, RCA Records; Ria Lewerke, United Artists Records; Dierdre Morrow, Island Records; Frank Mulvey, ABC Records; George Osaki, MCA Records; Ed Thrasher, Warner Bros. Records; Beverly Weinstein, Private Stock Records; and Roland Young, A&M Records. We would also like to thank Roger Ames at EMI, Jack Chudnoff at RCA Records, George Garabedian/Mark 56 Records, Dr. Ekke Schnabel at Polydor, and Marvin Schwartz at Capitol Records.

We wish to especially thank all the talented artists, designers and photographers whose creative efforts and support have been an inspiration to us: Lou Beach, Rod Dyer, Mick Haggerty, Dave McMacken, Peter Palombi, Neon Park, Norman Seeff, Bob Seidemann, John Van Hamersveld, Charlie White III, and Dave Willardson.

We gratefully thank all our friends who were involved in the production of this book: Warren Archer, Mike Mahoney and Gail Ryan at Color Service, J.B. at Angel Photo Color, Jim Ladwig at AGI in Chicago, and Jack Sklar at Ivy Hill Litho.

And to all our dear friends who have provided personal encouragement and support we wish to express very special thanks: Jon Sher, Bill Sayers, Fred Zax, Roger Black at Rolling Stone Magazine, Karl Bornstein at the Mirage Gallery, Bill Cohn, Woody Booséy, Maurice Boucher, and Joan Love Allemand.

There is a guy in Los Angeles who plans to market a framing kit so you can hang your favorite album covers on the wall.

Imagine that. In fact, imagine this book, an art book made up of record album covers. Nobody foresaw anything like this back in the fifties when they brought out the first long-play record "albums"—that Victorian word fragrant of sentiment and souvenirs. They called them albums because the record companies started making, in the 33⅓-rpm disk format, the equivalent of the 78-rpm albums, which were actually books of record sleeves (generally about eight) bound together. The 78 albums looked kind of like photo albums, and worked like them too, being basically a way of keeping your single records in one place. The first long-play albums had the same catchall quality.

Their covers were duller than cereal boxes, cheaply printed for the fifties look of cheesy elegance. There would be some writing to tell you what was inside the album jacket: short words, big letters. A photo or a bland commercial illustration. For classical music, maybe something *artistic* like an old painting—available at no expense from public domain, of course. The big exciting development in album covers as the fifties wore on was coy cheesecake. Album art looked as if it were designed to blend in with your furniture, be it blond maple, Naugahyde or Formica.

Or maybe it was actually meant to fit the music inside the album. With the A-Bomb and the Russians and Juvenile Delinquency to worry about, the fifties wanted bland, hope-for-the-best music. And got it. The art world, however, resisted the blandishments of mass culture.

It was a decade of brilliant experimentation in the visual arts, but of great isolation from the mainstream for the artists and their work. For years, for what seemed like eternities, artists and intellectuals sat over their wine and caffe espresso deploring the vulgarity of popular culture, and remaining at a haughty distance from it. The public was ignoring Abstract Expressionism and artists were lying low, thank you. As far as intellectuals were concerned, the American people had shown their true colors when Joseph McCarthy stirred up his anti-Red witch hunts and were therefore to be despised and ignored forever after.

The very bottom of the cultural heap, as far as *everybody* was concerned, was rock & roll. Even the rest of the vulgar popkulch looked down on it. And the last thing you'd ever hang on your wall, unless you were thirteen years old and had a crush on Elvis, was a rock & roll album cover. Rock albums were basically a way of remaindering old singles, maybe with a couple of hastily recorded filler tracks added, before the singer's flash died in the pan. The covers were rudimentary. Like the music.

While artists and intellectuals were groaning and deploring, the sixties dawned and suddenly there seemed to be something new in the air. There was Kennedy and Camelot and Pablo Casals playing at the White House. There was Pop Art and its teasing suggestion of…well, *fun* at the art gallery. Then there were the Mods, in England, where the nation least likely to discover fun was rocking & rolling.

Few knew it at the time, but here and there in the mix was a whiff of mind drugs. By the mid-sixties there was an aesthetically inclined rock and dope culture growing, soon to flower brilliantly in San Francisco. In that city a group of young people outside the hierarchy of the fine arts establishment was, half unconsciously, building a sandbox of its own. The Beatles had shown that rock & roll had room for personal expression and even (it sounded odd) taste. Some folk musicians began trying their hands at rock. The same phenomenon was happening elsewhere, too, but San Francisco was particularly lucky, because it had a live music scene which could support the rockers' experiments while building a powerful communion with the audience.

The dances at the Fillmore and Avalon ballrooms in San Francisco forged a group identity for the psychedelic crowd of a whole region. These dances became not just the social focus but the spiritual and even the intellectual focus of thousands of psychedelic tripsters. Bridging the gap between the new music and the old tired promotional art, a group of artists started creating some extraordinary posters to advertise the dances. In the crucible of this community's hopes, a graphic style—or rather, an approach to visual materials—was created which attempted a unity with the explorations of popular music.

The psychedelic experience was not so much a new experience as a new way of experiencing everything that exists. While musicians were ransacking folk, blues, jazz, Indian raga and electronic music for a vocabulary to express the inner adventures of being stoned, the poster artists were doing the same with all the world's art.

Technically the posters were simply advertising the dances, flashing their message for those who had eyes to see it: *Probably everybody is going to be stoned, join us.* But they became a subject of intense interest on their own. One day a dance promoter looked up after going down a block tacking up posters for that weekend's dance at the Fillmore Auditorium and saw somebody following him and taking them down. The promoter bowed to the inevitable and started printing enough posters to give away free at the dances.

The Fillmore posters evolved a style of heavy swirling lines with human faces or full nudes likely to appear anywhere in the flow; we see little of this kind of work today. The Avalon Ballroom hired a series of artists from Mouse Studios who were to have more influence on later developments. Mouse Studios developed an eclectic style characterized by elements of collage and gentle humor which set their work off from the swirling torment of the Fillmore posters, Rick Griffin, a one-time illustrator for Southern California surfer magazines, brought in a witty, metaphysical use of cartoon style and an all-American love for the iconography of commercial logos.

These new posters were not simply informational vehicles to be read and then discarded. They were part of an artistic and spiritual adventure of the most gripping sort. In the psychedelic apocalypse of 1967 they were subjected to minute scrutiny motivated by cosmic concerns. But even after the heaviest days of LSD use had passed, the habit of checking out art for its eyeball trips and cultural allusions continued — reinforced by the fact that after the Feds made it harder to manufacture LSD, the marijuana supply kept expanding. This aesthetic momentum found its full flowering long after psychedelia's early efforts.

A couple of things happened in 1967. It was the year (if you add a couple of months from 1966) that more LSD was made and consumed than in the twenty-four years since the first acid trip. It was also the year when phonograph records became, for the first time, a billion-dollar industry. The dominant sector of this market was rock & roll, but rock and its audience had both changed. Although AM radio was still playing three-minute singles, the public was buying albums. Amazingly, in 1967 for every 45-rpm single, six big expensive albums were sold. The age of the jukebox and the sock hop was over; the age of the stereo headphones had arrived.

The new albums, following the lead of the Beatles, were becoming more than a way of remaindering singles. They were more than "albums" now; they were designed with a total effect in mind and often a discernible unifying concept. The Beatles had included graphic design in their album conceptions at least as early as *Revolver,* the earliest album represented in this book. With *Sgt Pepper's Lonely Hearts Club Band* they set a standard that is still alive.

The new, Beatles-influenced musicians were mysterious and a little scary to the record companies, and the musicians sensed the power this gave them. With baffling disregard of the established way of doing business, they started making a kind of contract demand that was unheard of back in the days when rockers were considered lowlife incompetents. No longer were they to be processed like cold cuts by the all-powerful men from Artists and Repertoire. Starting with the Steve Miller Band, they asked for and received contracts that gave them big advances, plenty of time to experiment in the recording studio, a royalties formula that paid them by the minute rather than by the number of songs — adios to the three-minute song — and something called artistic control.

Artistic control meant being able to choose what songs you were going to play, what studio you would record in, and so on. It also meant a say in the design of your album package. The San Francisco bands naturally turned to their poster-making friends, and some continue that kind of family relationship today, like the Grateful Dead with Mouse Studios. Bands in other scenes sometimes had a particular artist who suited them: Neon Park, for example, has done a series of covers for Little Feat. But rock musicians everywhere wanted something more striking and personalized than record companies had been accustomed to giving.

A new million-dollar design industry has sprung up as a result. Record companies found that not only would the musicians raise trouble if the art was not right, but that record buyers were also becoming more demanding. Mere imitation — the usual way of dealing with new developments — was no longer enough. Established groups such as Jefferson Airplane or the J. Geils Band wanted striking, original gimmicks like the cover of *Bark* (packaged in a brown paper shopping bag) or the *Hotline* phone. Hoping not to miss a bet, the record companies often lavished elaborate design presentations on obscure groups as well; they still do.

The music and the art grew up together. For the more *organico* musicians, the art often stems from their personal life-styles. This can be anything from their dress (the Pointer Sisters' secondhand chic on *Steppin'*) or their debauched backstage habits (Rod Stewart's on-the-road boozing as portrayed on *Atlantic Crossing*), to much less literal, more stylized, metaphysicized signs for what they're up to (Leo Sayer's *Silver Bird,* Boz Scaggs' *Silk Degrees,* Pink Floyd's *Atom Heart Mother*). Sometimes the identity is so close that the musicians will buy the original art for their personal collections.

The "artistic freedom" insisted upon by today's musicians has resulted in the most striking commercial art — its dynamism deriving from the fact that it is, so to speak, art selling art, artists packaging artists. But as the musicians themselves are manic conglomerates of theatricality, eccentricity, virtuosity, talent and ego, accustomed to being the objects of intense (if fleeting) adulation from the public, this freedom has sometimes meant severe constraint for the artists. Brilliant designs may be rejected by the musicians for very subjective reasons, which is one explanation for why album art commissions are not as coveted as they might otherwise be, given the generally high fees. Fortunately a number of these orphan designs see the light of day for the first time in this book.

There is a West Coast bias to this collection, partly due to San Francisco's cultural influence and partly because Los Angeles, the center of the recording industry, has an art milieu of its own with a language of exuberant consumerism: cars and shopping centers and Disneyland and the surfing life.

But New York remains the fine arts center of the country and throughout the decade represented in this collection New York influences have been drifting in. The Art Deco wave is one, as is the related Art Decadence aura of sadomasochism that Andy Warhol's Pop Art scene still breathes. What's amazing is the ease with which L.A. whirls such things into merchandising. Underneath the whips and leather, you can still see the old pattern: the brittle, sophisticated East and the West with its ingratiating smile and terrific tan.

The current crop of à la mode graphic designers—whose record jackets are already a major influence in concept and package design—are former kids of the pacific fifties, educated in the turbulent sixties and matured in the eclectic, coming-together seventies. There is a kind of benevolent double-bind psychology about a cultural history like that, and it's evident in their most inventive creations.

On the one hand we find the nocturnal, Busby Berkeleyesque fantasies and chrome Oz's which speak so eloquently of the desire to return to more comforting eons, when ice cream dreams floated lazily up from pastel pillows while the orange bulb of a Zenith radio dial lighted a Fireside Chat. On the other, there is the harsher often vaguely sadomasochistic sexual imagery of the present, ranging from the (effective) emblematic airbrush vulgarities of Bill Imhoff's lips and tongue for Rufus to the sleazy motel rendezvous for Hummingbird—*We Can't Go On Meeting Like This.* And within the witty, risqué titles (*Is It In, Cheap Thrills, Let It Bleed, Schoolboys in Disgrace*), the spacey joy and slick malaise of our age are celebrated in this oddest of art collections: a book of pictures of packages for music circling back as Art.

Almost all the work in this book is the product of an aware group of art directors who are unique in their corporate power to give free rein to innovative, even controversial cover imagery by some of the finest available contemporary talent: great airbrush artists Robert Grossman, Peter Lloyd, Peter Palombi, Charles White III, and David Willardson, maverick semi-cartoonists Mick Haggerty and John Van Hamersveld, avant-garde photographers Moshe Brakha and Norman Seeff, and design firms such as AGI, Rod Dyer Inc., Gribbitt!, and Hipgnosis. The stuff is so good and varied some folks are known to buy the cover first, music second.

Any "fine arts" aura (in the conventional sense) to record jackets can be misleading; the covers are their own art-as-art form and derive very little cushioning, really, from the world of galleries and art magazines. Most art-world artists don't get the chance to do jackets. In the rare instance one does, it's a unique specimen like Andy Warhol (Paul Anka's *The Painter,* The Rolling Stones' *Sticky Fingers*), who's always had a foot in both camps (and who continually raises that hall-of-mirrors specter of Art-as-Popart-as-Art again).

Partial allusions to "fine art," however, are sketchily present. Peter Corriston's *Hotline* telephone for the J. Geils Band, and Bob Defrin's jacket for the Jan Hammer Group's *Oh Yeah?,* take a slight bow in the direction of Roy Lichtenstein's paintings (and Lichtenstein, incidentally, didn't invent the funky novelty-catalogue illustration, he only parodied it); Richard Amsel does a convincing turn on Toulouse-Lautrec with Maurice Chevalier; Peter Palombi exquisitely quotes Margaret Bourke-White's famous breadline photograph. And then there's Al Hirschfeld (Donald Byrd's *Caricatures*), the Broadway theatrical cartoonist who's earned almost enough hashmarks to be an Old Master.

Not all the jacket designs in this collection embellish the world of rock (there's some jazz, forties revival, and even a comedy and nostalgia platter or two), but the flavor is pervasive, and the designs reflect it. No traces at all of the old fifties "LP"—pink-and-black bowling alley lettering, the plasterers hint at Abstract Expression (for the jazz set), or a bosomy girl reclining in (for no discernible reason) harem pajamas. No supermarket shelf at $1.99. No fusty, dignified, moribund Deutschegramaphone profundity. And certainly no tiny, isolated, philatelic audience.

Because rock music is such a monumental socio-cultural force in America, the English-speaking world and beyond, huge quantities of albums are released, each with its own enigmatic title, identifiable look and appeal to each individual (albeit not sequestered) corner of the market: dope, sci-fi, nostalgia, symphonic rock, European synthesizer, period camp, heavy metal, quasi-folk, soul and Texas outlaw. In this onslaught every graphic arrow is loosed—sex, sentiment, optical conundrums, exhumations of old auntie artifacts like orange crate label art, and Surrealist free association.

The physical techniques are myriad: Norman Seeff's eerily straight photography, photo-montage (which the rock industry, with its massive production budgets, does *right*—the best stuff since John Heartfield's Weimar Republic anti-Nazi broadsides), tinted photos (like Bob Cato's and John Kehe's for Electric Light Orchestra), *trompe-l'oeil* realism like Dave McMacken's for *Tom Cat,* Lou Beach's collage/montage, typography reminiscent of the best of the twenties and thirties when graphic designs were built like the perennial brick shithouse (Humble Pie's *Smokin'*), and of course the ubiquitous airbrush, which rock album cover art revived virtually single-handedly in the last decade.

One big difference between commercial art (and here it's the very best) and fine art is the constant plundering of previous aesthetics; commercial art recycles like nobody's business. (The public possesses by now an ingrained graphic awareness which can be played on, owing to a few decades of inundation with design jewels like Coca Cola, Campbell's Soups, CBS, McDonalds and Revlon).

Moreover, the new music is ripe with its own chronicle—from the historic but cheaply produced San Francisco posters in the halcyon flower-child years, from light shows, psychedelia and the peace movement. Added to this electric compost are shovelsful of Disneyesque and Looneytoonful drawing, Maxfield Parrish memorabilia, a wholesale resurrection of Art Nouveau and Art Deco, and odes to Fred Astaire and Raymond Chandler which bespeak an overwhelming urge to believe, once more, that "smart" is *smart.* The bloom is archive rather than icon, a rich catalogue of art and social history. If academics knew what they were doing, this collection would be the survey textbook.

The jackets boast, nevertheless, a rich milepost row of their own. The oldest cover in the book, the Beatles' *Revolver,* is a precursor of the jacket (and album) that made rock respectable, even *de rigueur,* among the intelligentsia: *Sgt Pepper's Lonely Hearts Club Band.* After those are paraded the memorable, wonderfully distasteful Stones covers (*Let It Bleed, Sticky Fingers,* and *Made In The Shade*), the infamous semi-censored Blind Faith pubescent nude by Bob Seidemann—the inoffensive cover offered as an alternative has ironically become the rarer version—Neon Park's grating, flesh-ripping weasel razor for the Mothers of Invention, the kinky chrome bathroom fantasy created by Hipgnosis for UFO-*Force It,* Moshe Brakha's great fleeting photograph on Richie Havens' *The End of the Beginning,* Richard Amsel's classic portrait of *The Divine Miss M,* the Ohio Players' phallic and seminal *Fire* and *Honey,* the Byrds' appropriation of folk artist Jo Mora's *Sweetheart of the Rodeo,* Robert Crumb's prime funk comic on *Cheap Thrills,* Bob Zoell's Looneytoon style *Flamin' Groovies,* David Willardson's pop parody of Little Richard and Marilyn Monroe, and John Berg's Grammy award-winning unwrapped Hersheybar concept for Chicago.

Only image scores in this business. No integrity points for virgin originality. Anything goes, anything counts, and all allusions are hereby eliminated from annoying (and senseless) pedigree squabbles. Given these impossible demands, the artists, designers, and art directors on these record jackets continue to compose symphonies in the furnace.

—Charles Perry and Peter Plagens

Charles Perry is an editor of Rolling Stone Magazine *and the author of a forthcoming history of the Haight-Ashbury. Peter Plagens is an artist and the author of* Sunshine Muse: Contemporary Art on the West Coast.

Zephyr: Sunset Ride
Artist: David Willardson/Star Studios
Logo Design: John Casado
Art Director: Ed Thrasher
Date: 1972 Warner Bros. Records

Pink Floyd — Atom Heart Mother
Cover Design and Art Direction: Hipgnosis
Date: 1969 Harvest Records (Capitol EMI)

Flamin' Groovies — Supersnazz
Artist: Bob Zoell
Design: Richard Mantel
Art Direction: John Berg
Date: 1969 Epic Records

This is Helen O'Connell

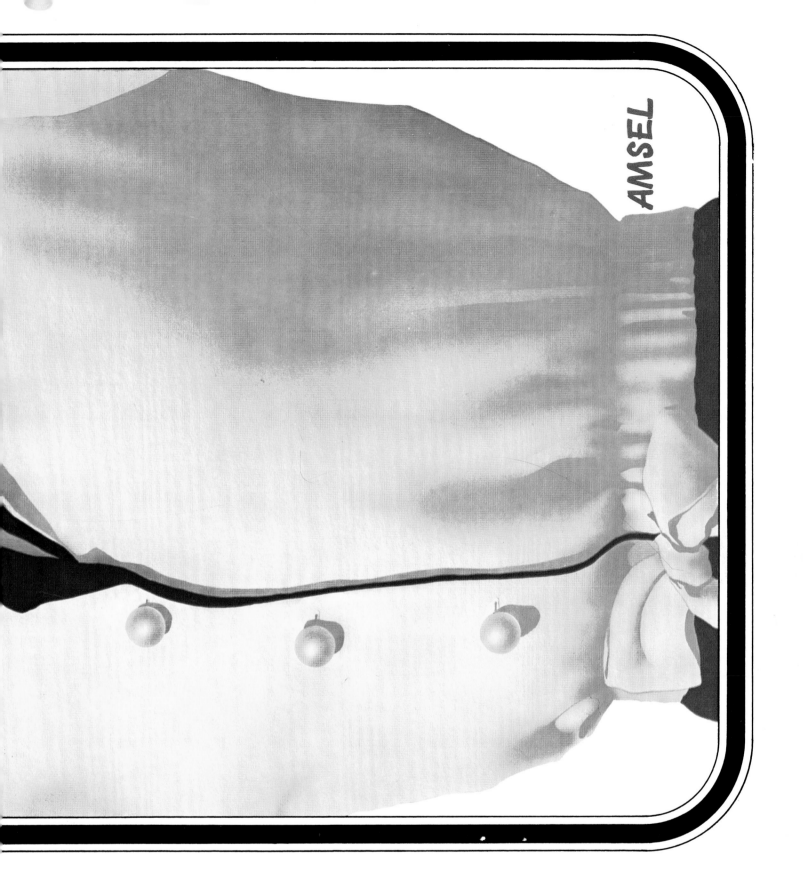

This Is Helen O'Connell
Artist: Richard Amsel
Art Direction: Acy Lehman
Date: 1972 RCA Records

Bang! Music
Design: Mick Haggerty/Rod Dyer Inc.
Art Direction: John Hoernle
Date: 1973 Capitol Records

Blind Faith
Photography and Art Direction: Bob Seidemann
Date: 1969 Atco Records

Boz Scaggs — Silk Degrees
Cover and inner sleeve photography: Moshe Brakha
Art Direction: Ron Coro and Nancy Donald
Date: 1976 Columbia Records

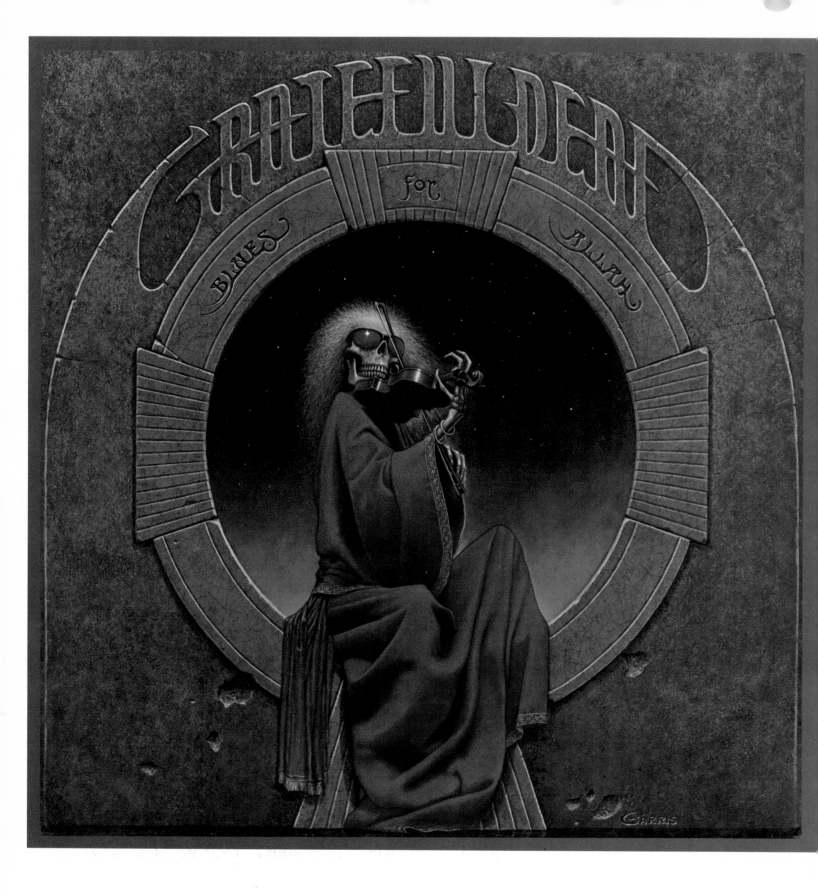

Grateful Dead — Blues for Allah
Artist: Philip Garris
Art Direction: Ria Lewerke
Date: 1975 United Artists Records

Humble Pie — Smokin'
Artist: Richard Eckford
Logo Design: John Kosh
Art Direction: Mike Doud
Date: 1972 A&M Records

Jan Hammer Group — Oh Yeah?
Art Direction: Bob Defrin
Date: 1976 Nemperor Records

Blackfoot — No Reservations
Art, Concept and Design: Mick Haggerty
Art Direction: Susan Markheim
Date: 1976 Island Records

J. Geils Band — Hotline
Cover Concept and Design: Peter Corriston / AGI
Date: 1975 Atlantic Records

Golden Summer
Artist: Jim Evans
Design and Art Direction: Ria Lewerke
Date: 1976 United Artists Records

Little Richard — Second Coming
Artist: David Willardson/Star Studios
Art Director: Ed Thrasher
Date: 1972 Warner Bros. Records

Unpublished Work
Artist: David Willardson/Star Studios
Art Direction: Frank Mulvey
Date: 1973

23

The Tubes
Front Cover Photography: Harry Mittman
Back Cover Photography: Ian Patrick
Concept and Design: Airamid Designs, M. Cotton, P. Prince
Logo Design: Richard Seireeni
Art Direction: Roland Young
Date: 1975 A&M Records

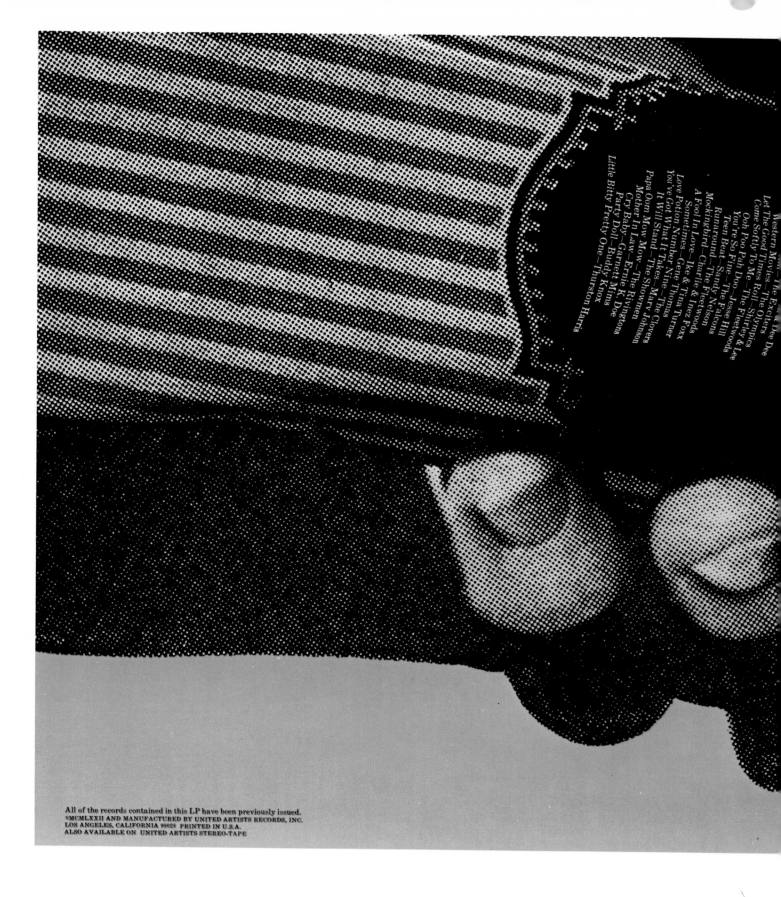

...estern Movies—The Exciters
Dee Dee
Let The Good Times Roll—Shirley & Lee
Come Softly To Me—The Fleetwoods
Ooh Poo Pah Doo—Jesse Hill
You're So Fine—The Falcons
Teen Beat—Sandy Nelson
Runaround—The Fleetwoods
Mockingbird—Charlie & Inez Foxx
A Fool In Love—Ike & Tina Turner
Sometimes—Gene Thomas
Love Potion Number Nine—The Clovers
You've Got What It Takes—Marv Johnson
It Will Stand—The Showmen
Papa Oom Mow Mow—The Rivingtons
Mother In Law—Ernie K. Doe
Cry Baby—Garnett Mims
Party Doll—Buddy Knox
Little Bitty Pretty One—Thurston Harris

Monaural. Can be played on stereo equipment. ©MCMLXXII UNITED ARTISTS RECORDS, INC.

Greasy Kid's Stuff
Artist: Rod Dyer
Art Direction: Norman Seeff
Date: 1972 United Artists Records

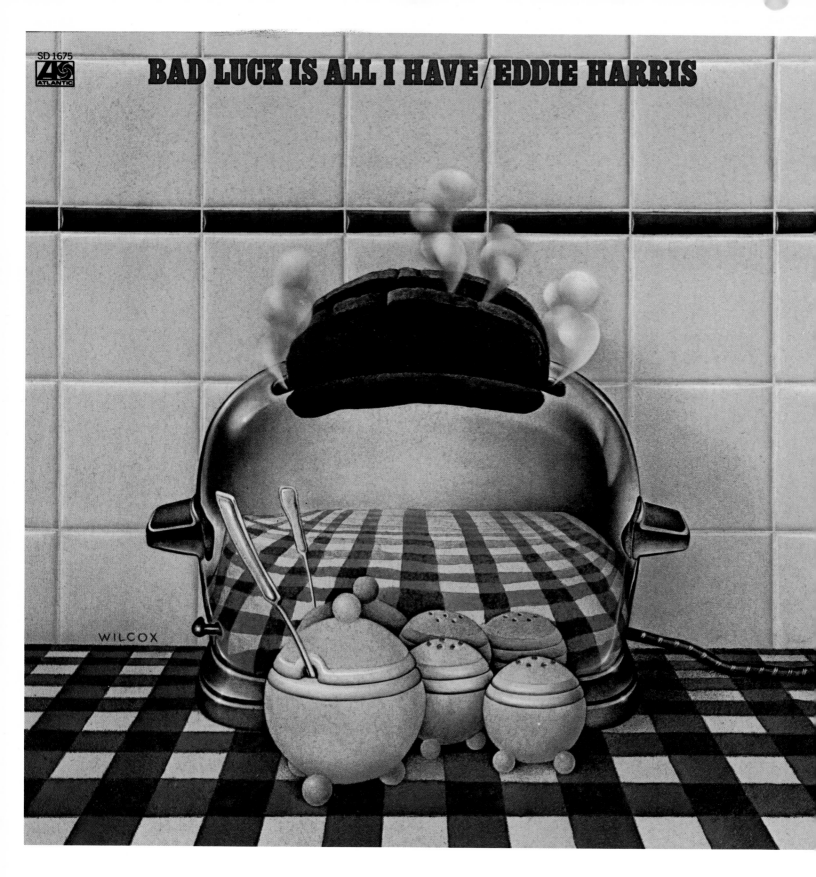

BAD LUCK IS ALL I HAVE / EDDIE HARRIS

WILCOX

Eddie Harris — Bad Luck Is All I Have
Artist: Dave Wilcox
Art Direction: Bob Defrin and Paula Scher
Date: 1975 Atlantic Records

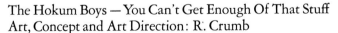

The Hokum Boys — You Can't Get Enough Of That Stuff
Art, Concept and Art Direction: R. Crumb
Date: 1975 Yazoo Records

Target
Artist: Lou Beach
Art Direction: Roland Young
Date: 1976 A&M Records

Country Joe and The Fish — Here We Go Again
Art and Design: Tom Weller
Art Direction: Jules Halfant
Date: 1969 Vanguard Records

Unpublished Work
Artist: David Willardson/Star Studios
Art Direction: Mike Salisbury
Date: 1973

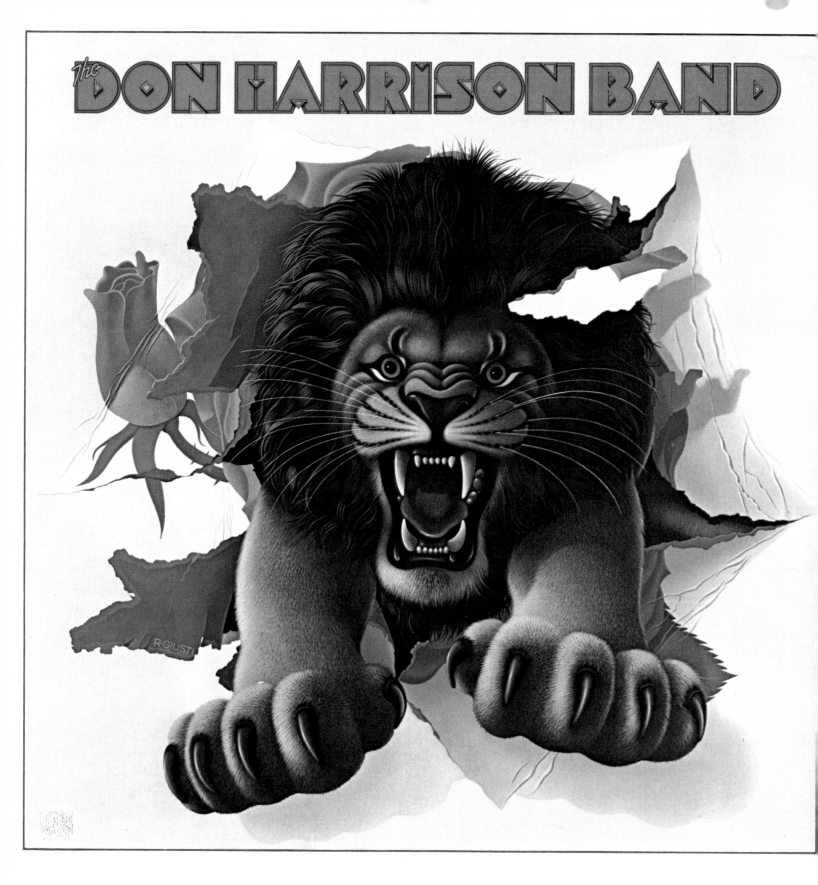

The Don Harrison Band
Artist: Robert Giusti
Art Direction: Bob Defrin and Abie Sussman
Date: 1976 Atlantic Records

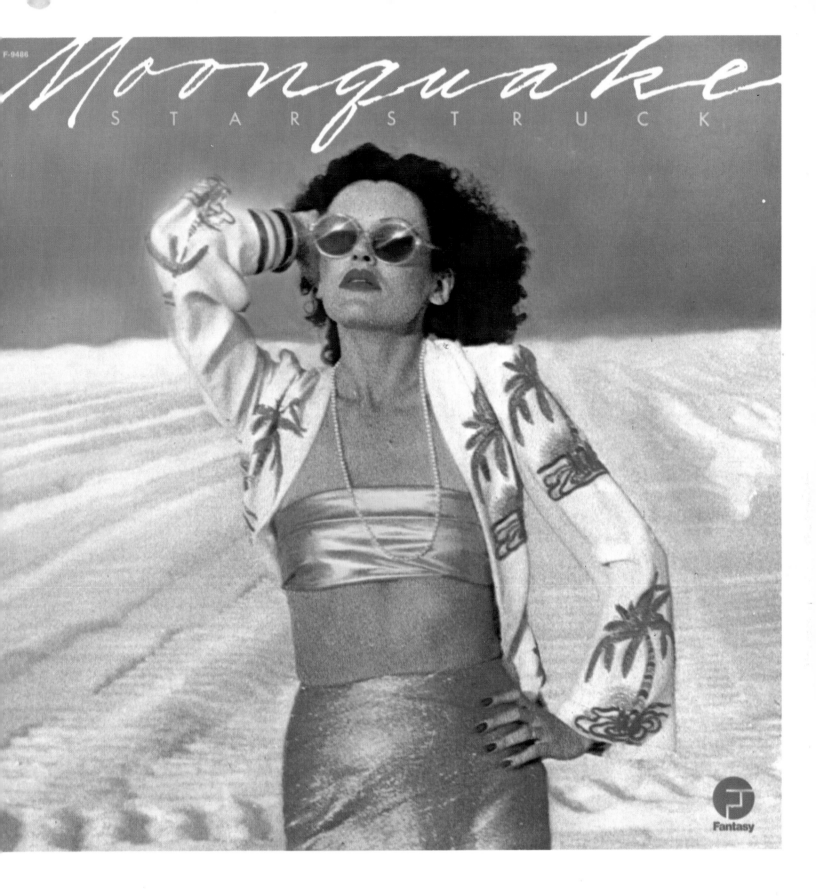

Moonquake — Starstruck
Photography: Elizabeth Lennard
Art Direction: Phil Carroll
Date: 1975 Fantasy Records

Disco Cover
Photography & Design: Richard Seireeni/Rod Dyer, Inc.
Date: 1977 Warner Bros. Records

Jefferson Starship — Dragonfly
Artist: Peter Lloyd
Art Direction: Frank Mulvey and Acy Lehman
Date: 1974 Grunt Records

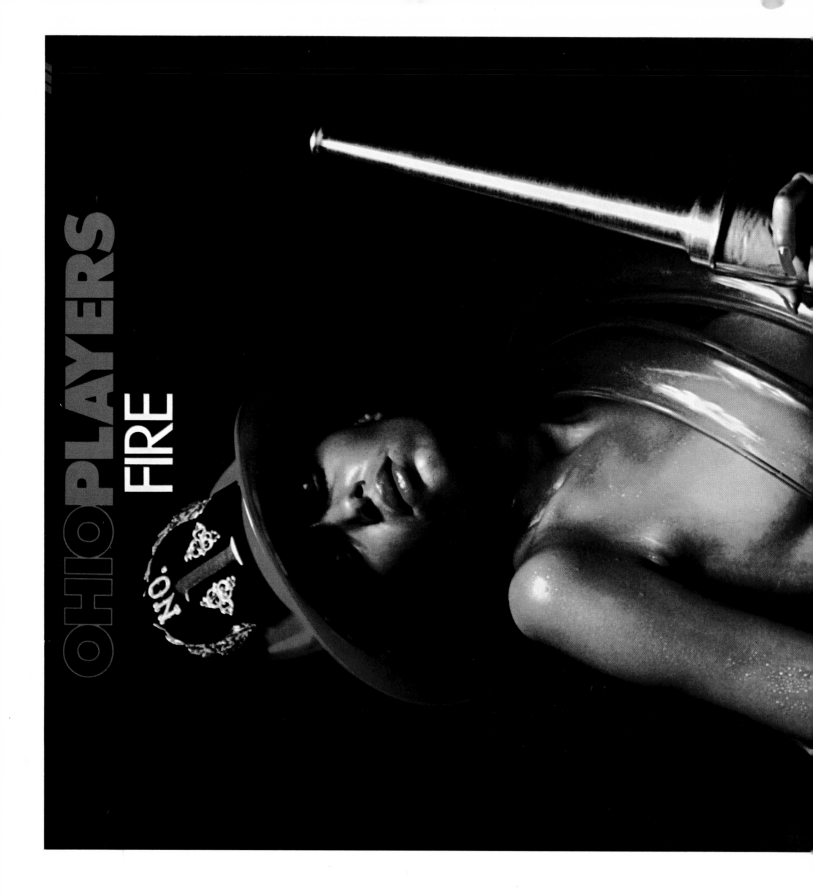

FIRE
TOGETHER
RUNNIN' FROM THE DEVIL
I WANT TO BE FREE
SMOKE
IT'S ALL OVER
WHAT THE HELL
TOGETHER (REPRISE)

The Ohio Players — Fire
Photography: Stan Malinowski
Design: Len Willis/Gnu World
Art Direction: Jim Ladwig/AGI
Date: 1975 Mercury Records

Bonzo Dog Band — Beast of the Bonzos
Artist: John Van Hamersveld
Concept: Martin Cerf and John Mendelsohn
Art Direction: Norman Seeff
Date: 1971 United Artists Records

AVR-9200

Beans
Artist: John Van Hamersveld
Concept and Art Direction: John Van Hamersveld
Date: 1972 Avalanche/United Artists Records

SIDE I
WASTED WORDS
SOUTHBOUND
RAMBLIN' MAN

SIDE II
IN MEMORY OF
ELIZABETH REED

SIDE III
AIN'T WASTIN' TIME NO MORE
COME AND GO BLUES
CAN'T LOSE WHAT
YOU NEVER HAD

SIDE IV
DON'T WANT YOU NO MORE
IT'S NOT MY CROSS TO BEAR
JESSICA

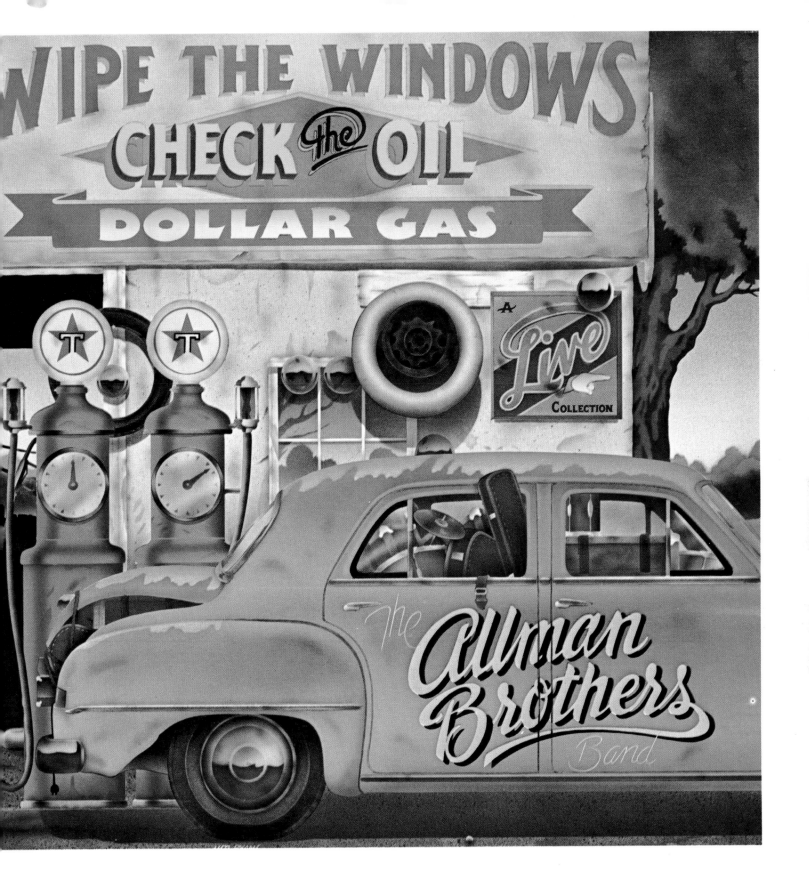

The Allman Brothers Band —Wipe The Windows,
Check The Oil, Dollar Gas
Art and Design: Jim Evans
Art Direction: Diana Kaylan
Date: 1976 Capricorn Records

Nils Lofgren
Photography: Ed Caraeff
Design: Junie Osaki
Art Direction: Roland Young
Date: 1975 A&M Records

Starcastle
Artist: Alex Ebel
Art Direction: Ed Lee
Date: 1976 Epic Records

Universal Sleeve — A&M Records
Artist: Brian Hagiwara/Rod Dyer Inc.
Art Direction: Roland Young
Date: 1975 A&M Records

Sweathog
Artist: Bill Imhoff
Design and Art Direction: John Berg and Virginia Team
Date: 1971 Columbia Records

Contemporary Sampler
Artist: John Mattos
Design and Art Direction: Ria Lewerke
Date: 1976 Blue Note Records

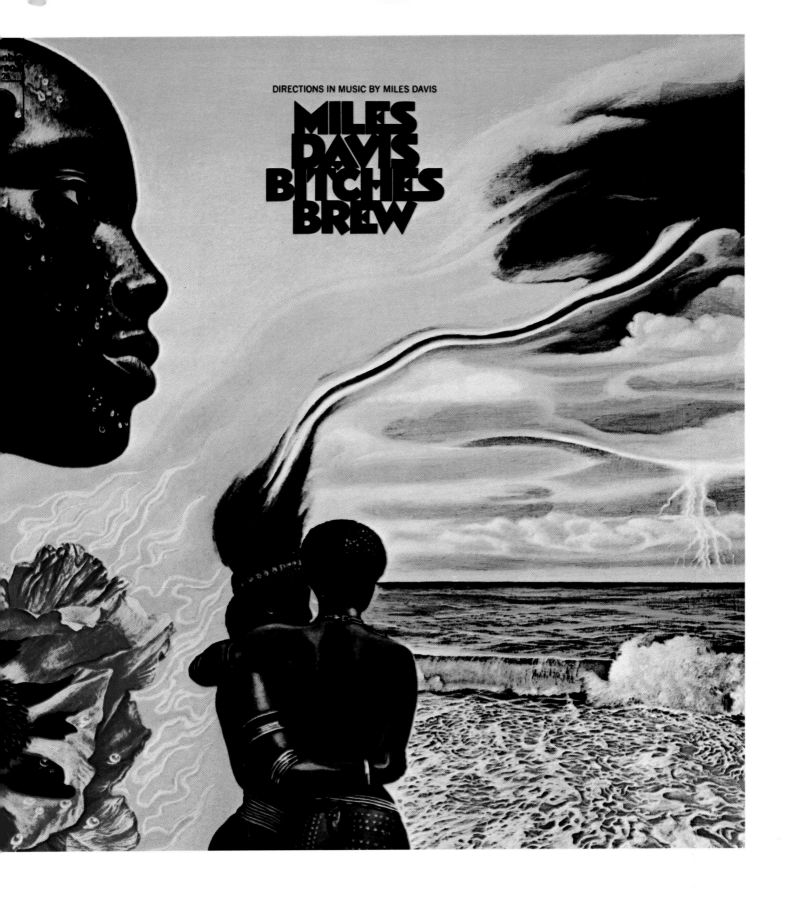

Miles Davis — Bitches Brew
Artist: Mati Klarwein
Art Direction: John Berg
Date: 1970 Columbia Records

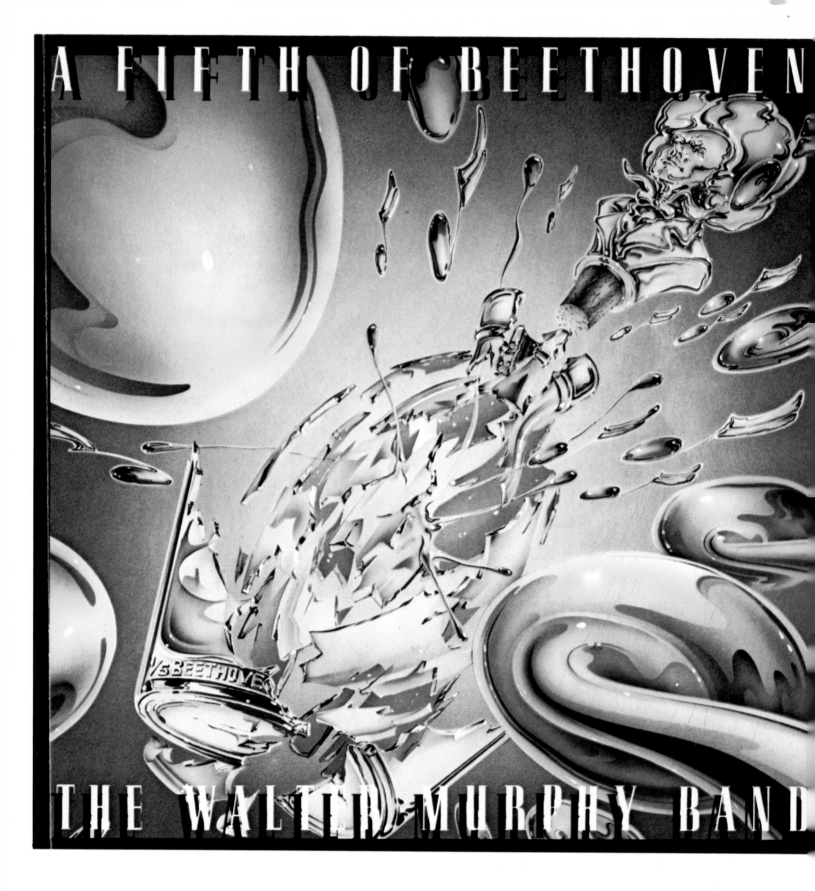

The Walter Murphy Band — A Fifth of Beethoven
Artist: Bob Hickson
Concept and Design: John Kosh
Date: 1976 Private Stock Records

Electric Light Orchestra — Eldorado
Concept: John Kehe
Art Direction: Bob Cato
Date: 1974 United Artists Records

Curtis Mayfield — There's No Place Like America Today
Artist: Peter Palombi
Art Direction: Ed Thrasher
Date: 1975 Curtom Records

The James Montgomery Band
Artist: Mick Haggerty
Design Concept: Mike Fink/Rod Dyer Inc.
Art Direction: Deirdre Morrow
Date: 1977 Island Records

Rufus — Featuring Chaka Khan
Artist: Bill Imhoff
Design: Bill Naegels/Rod Dyer
Art Direction: Frank Mulvey
Date: 1975 ABC Records

The Pointer Sisters — Steppin'
Artist: Joe Heiner/Star Studios
Packaging Concept: Bob Weiner
Design and Art Direction: Mick Haggerty/Art Attack
Date: 1975 ABC Records

Mott The Hoople — Rock and Roll Queen
Artist: Philip Castle
Cover Design: Eckford/Stimpson
Date: 1974 Atlantic Records

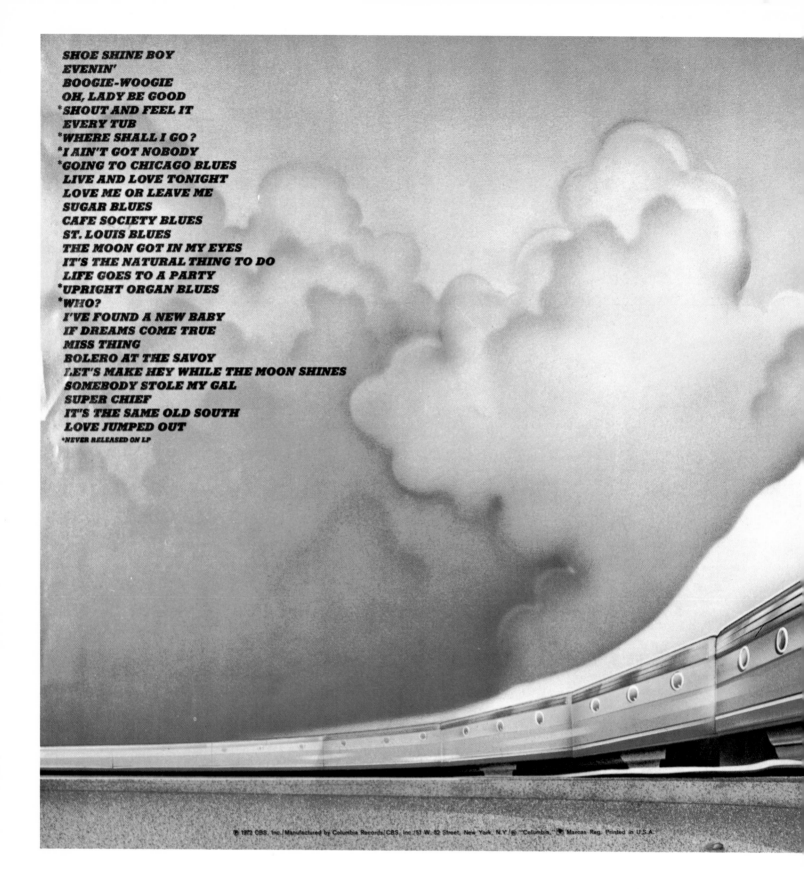

SHOE SHINE BOY
EVENIN'
BOOGIE-WOOGIE
OH, LADY BE GOOD
*SHOUT AND FEEL IT
EVERY TUB
*WHERE SHALL I GO?
*I AIN'T GOT NOBODY
*GOING TO CHICAGO BLUES
LIVE AND LOVE TONIGHT
LOVE ME OR LEAVE ME
SUGAR BLUES
CAFE SOCIETY BLUES
ST. LOUIS BLUES
THE MOON GOT IN MY EYES
IT'S THE NATURAL THING TO DO
LIFE GOES TO A PARTY
*UPRIGHT ORGAN BLUES
*WHO?
I'VE FOUND A NEW BABY
IF DREAMS COME TRUE
MISS THING
BOLERO AT THE SAVOY
LET'S MAKE HEY WHILE THE MOON SHINES
SOMEBODY STOLE MY GAL
SUPER CHIEF
IT'S THE SAME OLD SOUTH
LOVE JUMPED OUT
*NEVER RELEASED ON LP

Count Basie — Super Chief
Art and Design: David Willardson/Star Studios
Concept and Art Direction: John Berg
Date: 1972 Columbia Records

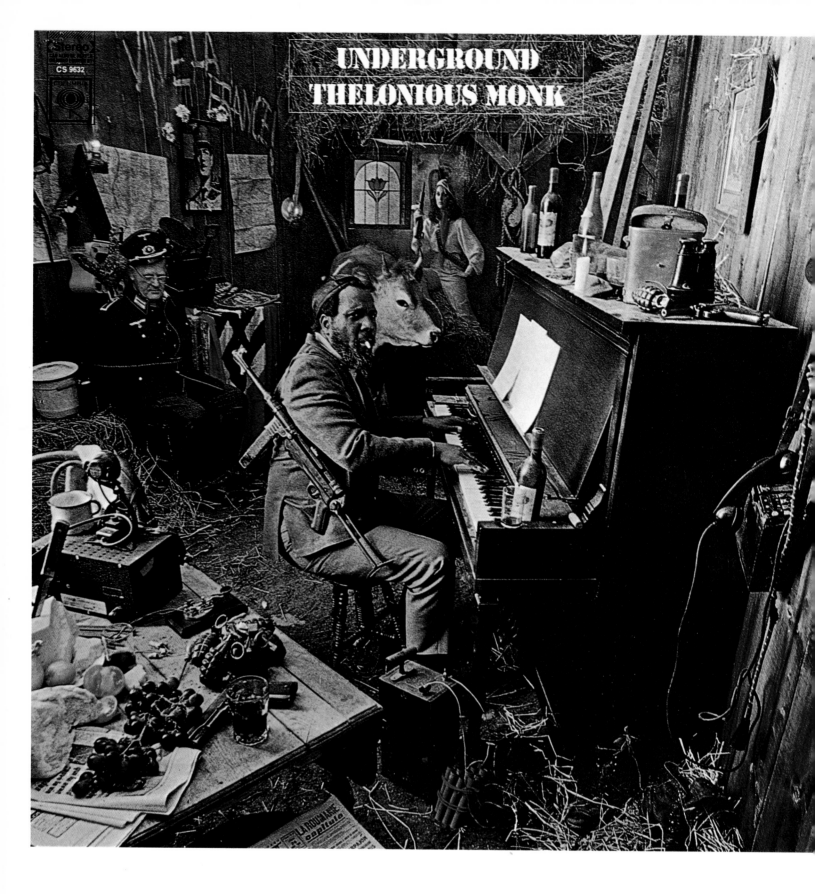

Thelonius Monk — Underground
Photography: Horn/Griner
Concept and Design: John Berg and Richard Mantel
Art Direction: John Berg
Date: 1968 Columbia Records

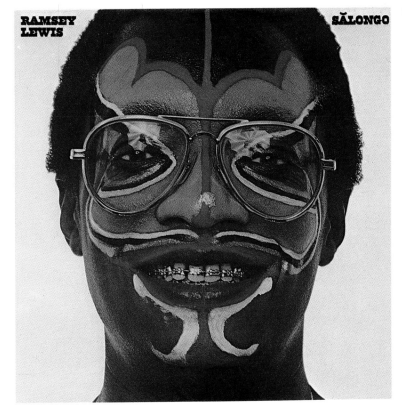

The Byrds — Byrdmaniax
Life Masks: Mary Leonard
Concept: John Berg
Design and Art Direction: John Berg and Virginia Team
Date: 1971 Columbia Records

Santana — Greatest Hits
Photography: Joel Baldwin
Concept and Design: John Berg
Date: 1974 Columbia Records

The Dynamic Superiors — Give and Take
Photography: Howard Deshong
Concept and Design: Snyder/Butler Advertising
Graphics Coordination: Carl Overr
Date: 1977 Motown Records

Ramsey Lewis — Salongo
Photography: Norman Seeff
Make-up by Natasha
Design and Art Direction: John Berg and Paula Scher
Date: 1976 Columbia Records

Chicago X
Artist: Nick Fasciano
Concept, Design and Art Direction: John Berg
Date: 1976 Columbia Records

The Sidewalks of New York
Artist: Robert Grossman
Design and Art Direction: Paula Chwast
Date: 1976 Columbia Records

Cecilio and Kapono
Artist: David Willardson/Star Studios
Logo Design: Mike Schwab
Concept and Art Direction: Ron Coro
Date: 1974 Columbia Records

Pretty Things — Silk Torpedo
Cover Art: Hipgnosis
Color Work: Richard Manning
Date: 1974 Swan Song (Atlantic) Records

Peace & Quiet

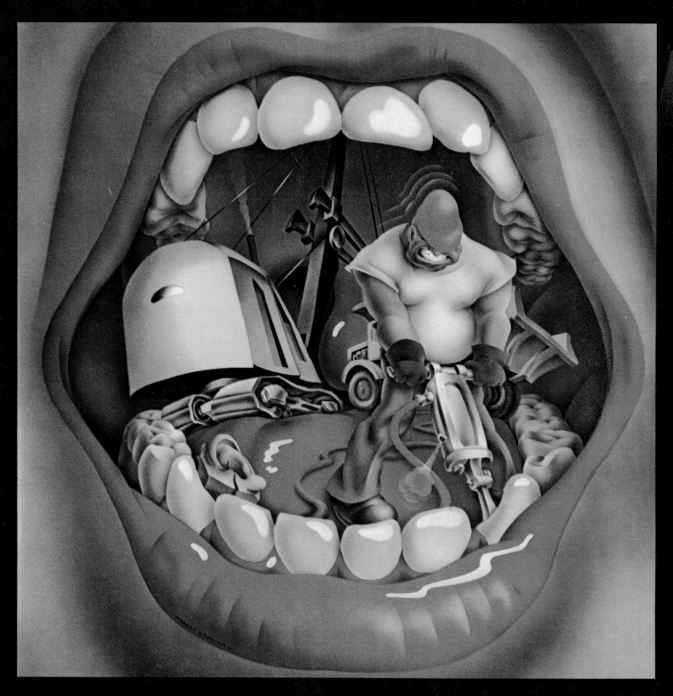

Peace and Quiet
Artist: Robert Grossman
Design: Henrietta Condak
Art Direction: John Berg
Date: 1970 Kinetic Records

Big Brother and the Holding Co.— Cheap Thrills
Artist: R. Crumb
Art Direction: John Berg
Date: 1968 Columbia Records

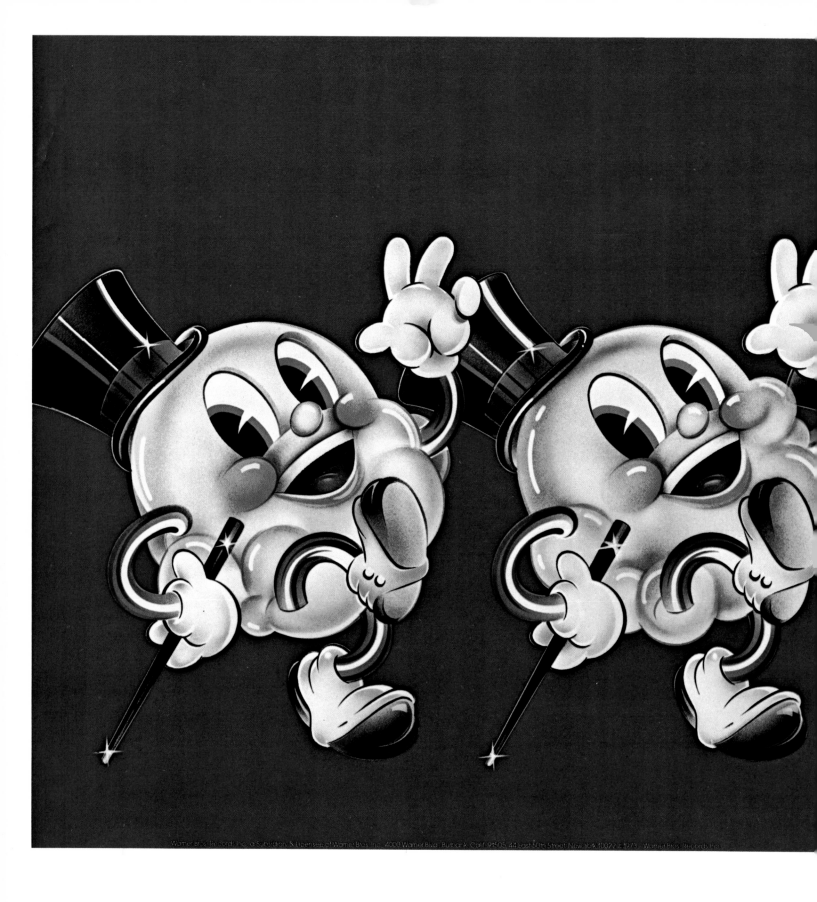

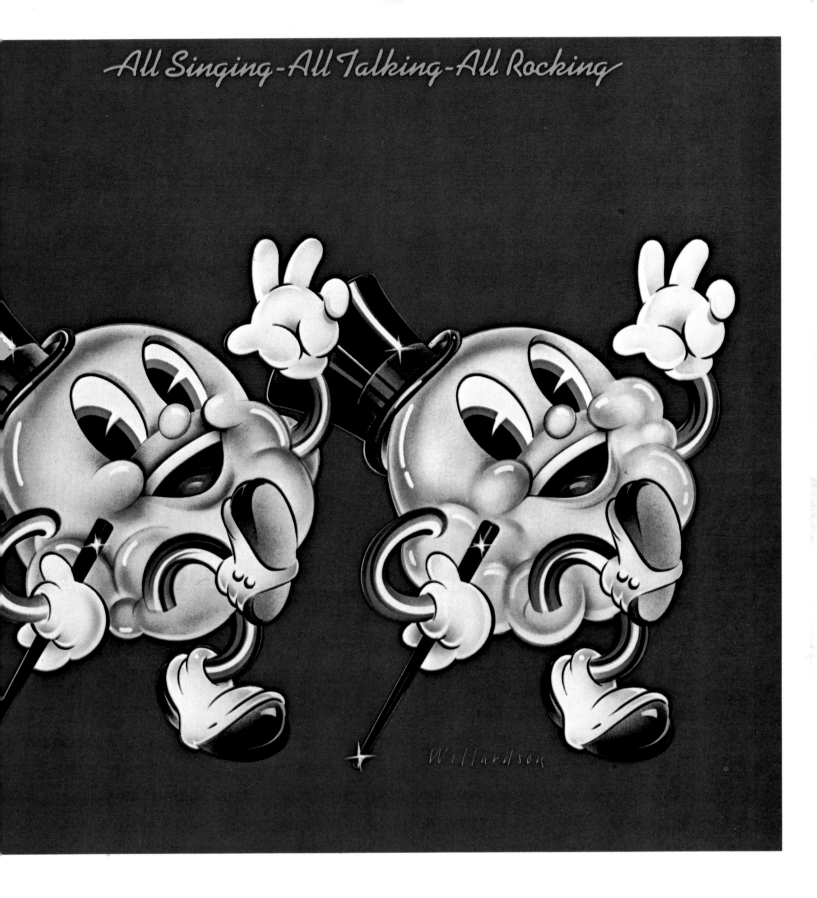

All Singing, All Talking, All Rocking
Artist: David Willardson/Star Studios
Design and Art Direction: John Casado
Date: 1974 Warner Bros. Records

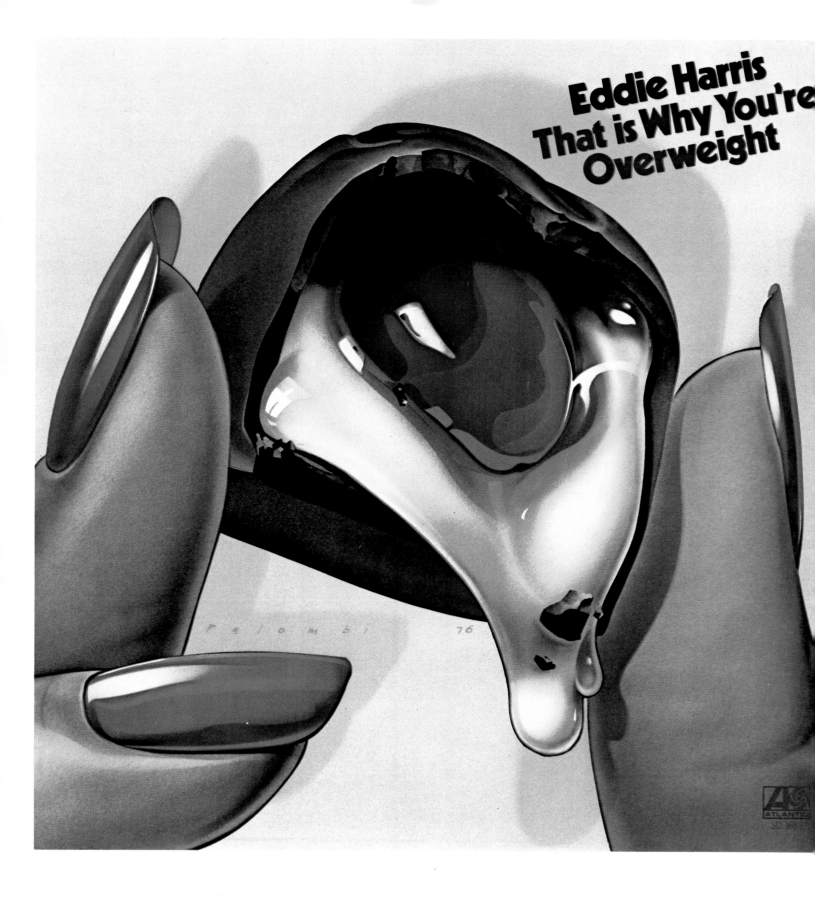

Eddie Harris — That Is Why You're Overweight
Artist: Peter Palombi
Art Direction: Bob Defrin and Lynn Breslin
Date: 1976 Atlantic Records

Freddie King — Larger Than Life
Artist: Karen Katz
Photography: Larry Couzens
Art Direction: Bob Defrin and Abie Sussman
Date: 1975 R.S.O. Records

Jerry Lee Lewis

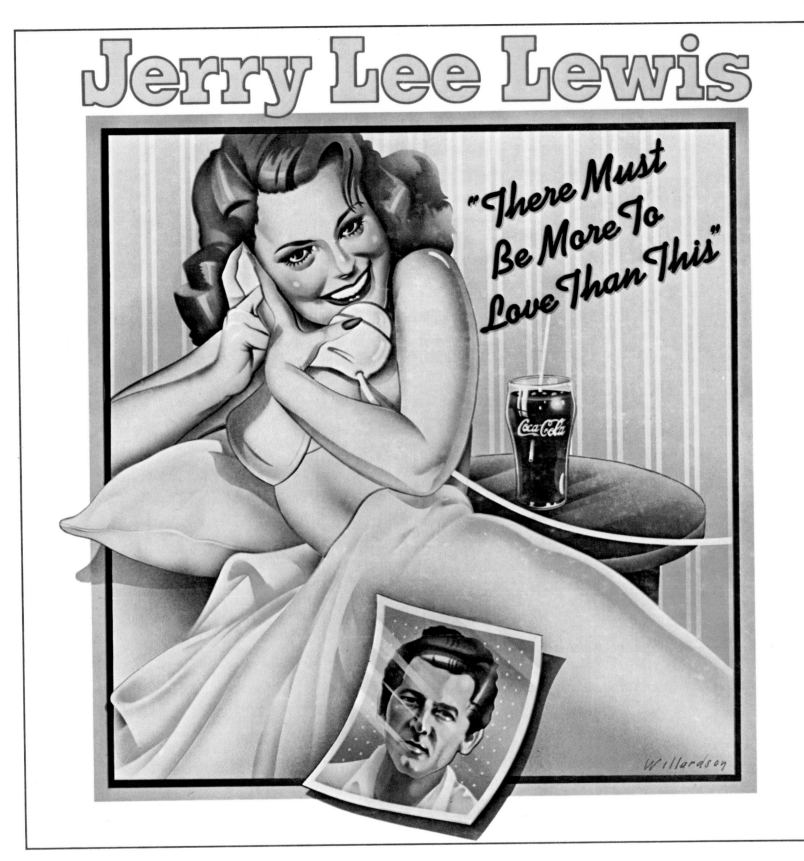

"There Must Be More To Love Than This"

Jerry Lee Lewis —There Must Be More To Love Than This
Artist: David Willardson/Star Studios
Concept: David Willardson and Des Strobel
Logo Design: John Van Hamersveld
Date: 1971 Mercury Records

Dick Powell in Hollywood
Design: Miles Kreuger and Nereus Bell
Art Direction: John Berg and Virginia Team
Date: 1968 Columbia Records

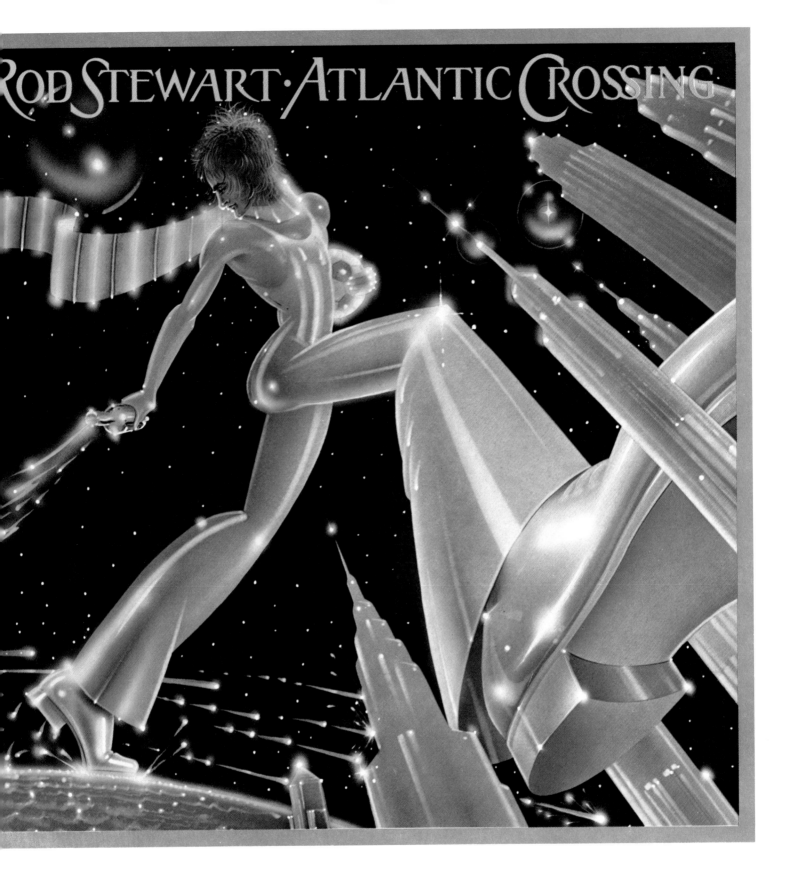

Rod Stewart — Atlantic Crossing
Artist: Peter Lloyd
Art Preparation: AGI, Hollywood
Design and Art Direction: John Kosh
Date: 1975 Warner Bros. Records

Jefferson Airplane — Bark
Photography: Mick Sangiamo
Concept and Art Direction: Acy Lehman
Date: 1971 Grunt Records

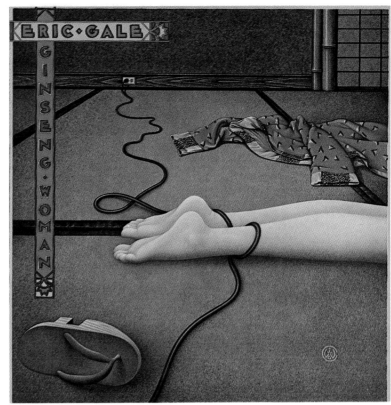

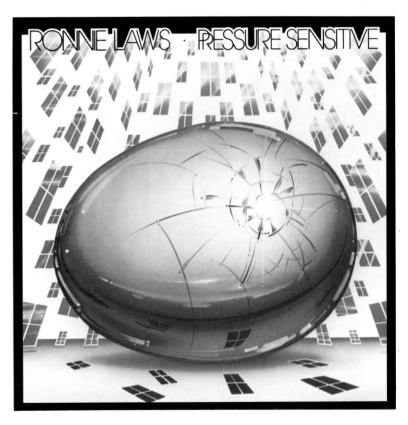

Boulez — Le Sacre du Printemps
Artist: Guy Billout
Art Direction: John Berg
Date: 1970 Columbia Records

Eric Gale — Ginseng Woman
Artist: Dave Wilcox
Design: Paula Scher and Andy Engel
Art Direction: Paula Scher
Date: 1977 Columbia Records

Kinky Friedman — Lasso From El Paso
Artist: John Kehe
Design: John Kehe and Tom Steele
Art Direction: Tom Steele
Date: 1976 Columbia Records

Ronnie Laws — Pressure Sensitive
Artist: Peter Lloyd
Design and Art Direction: Bob Cato
Date: 1975 Blue Note Records

Flo and Eddie — Moving Targets
Artist: Dave McMacken
Design: Ron Coro and Dave McMacken
Art Direction: Ron Coro
Date: 1976 Columbia Records

Weather Report — Heavy Weather
Artist: Lou Beach
Art Direction: Nancy Donald
Date: 1976 Columbia Records

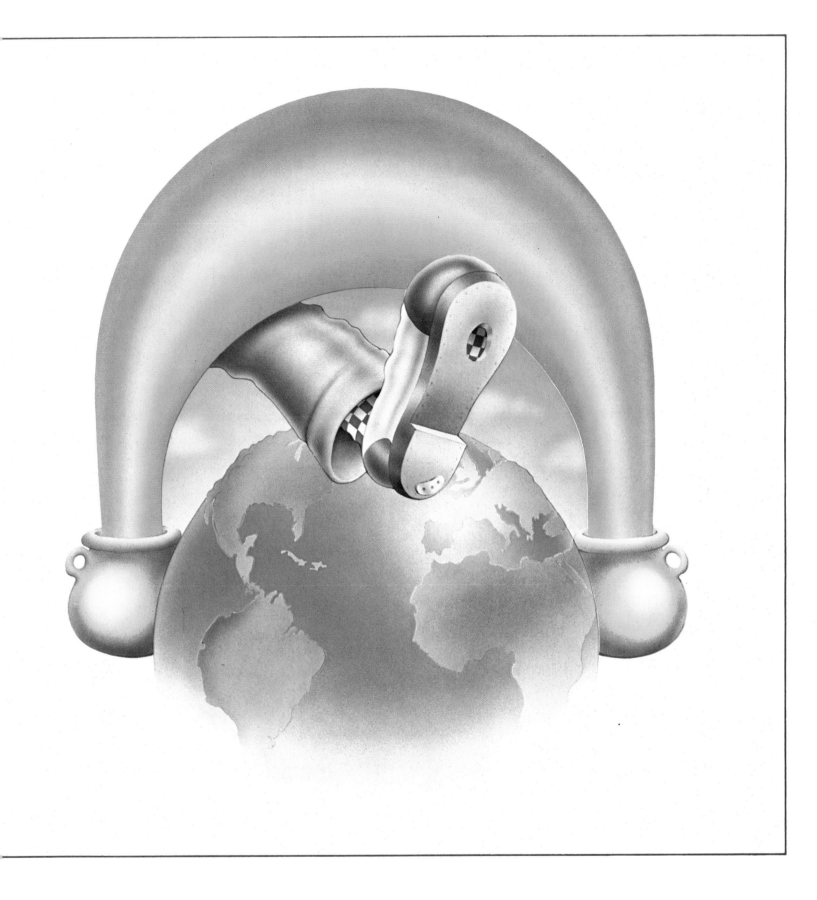

Grateful Dead — Europe '72
Art and Concept: Kelley/Mouse Studios
Art Direction: Ed Thrasher
Date: 1972 Warner Bros. Records

Unpublished Work
Artist: David Willardson/Star Studios
Art Direction: John Casado
Date: 1974

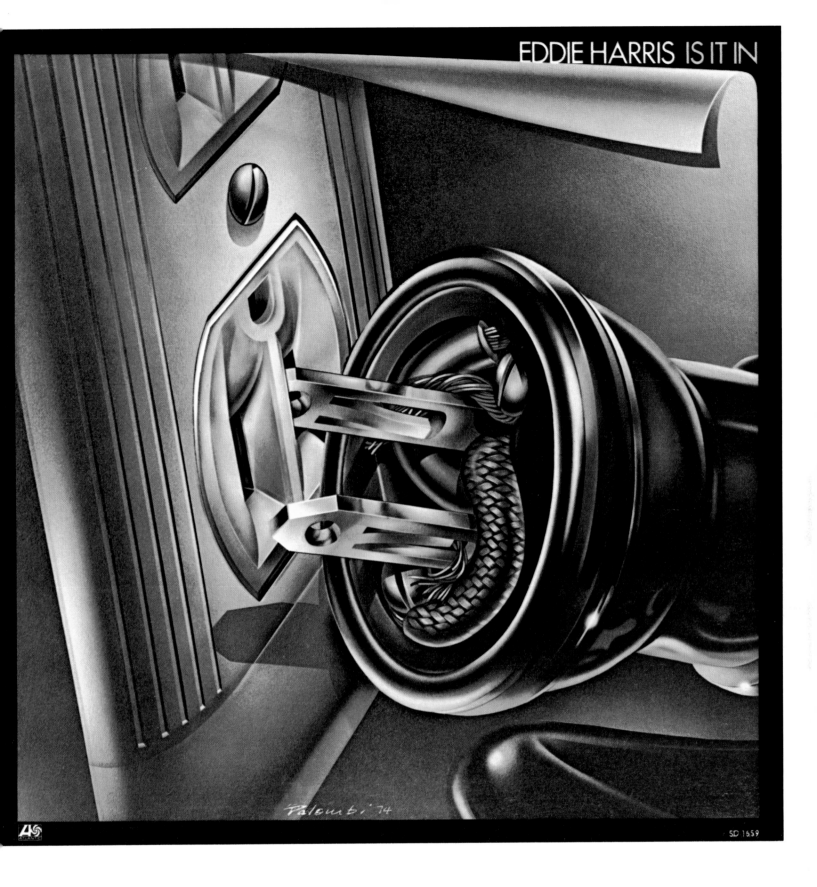

Eddie Harris — Is It In
Artist: Peter Palombi
Art Direction: Bob Defrin and Basil Pao
Date: 1974 Atlantic Records

Unpublished Work
Artist: Lou Beach
Art Direction: Frank Mulvey
Date: 1974

Leo Sayer — Silver Bird
Photography and Concept: Graham Hughes
Date: 1973 Chrysalis/Warner Bros. Records

The Rolling Stones—Made In The Shade
Artist: Christian Piper
Date: 1976 Rolling Stones Records

Little Feat — Dixie Chicken
Artist: Neon Park
Art Direction: Ed Thrasher
Date: 1973 Warner Bros. Records

The Steve Miller Band — Book of Dreams
Artist: Kelley and Mouse
Art Direction: Roy Kohara
Date: 1977 Capitol Records

American Graffiti
Artist: David Willardson/Star Studios
Logo Design: John Casado
Art Direction: George Osaki
Date: 1973 MCA Records

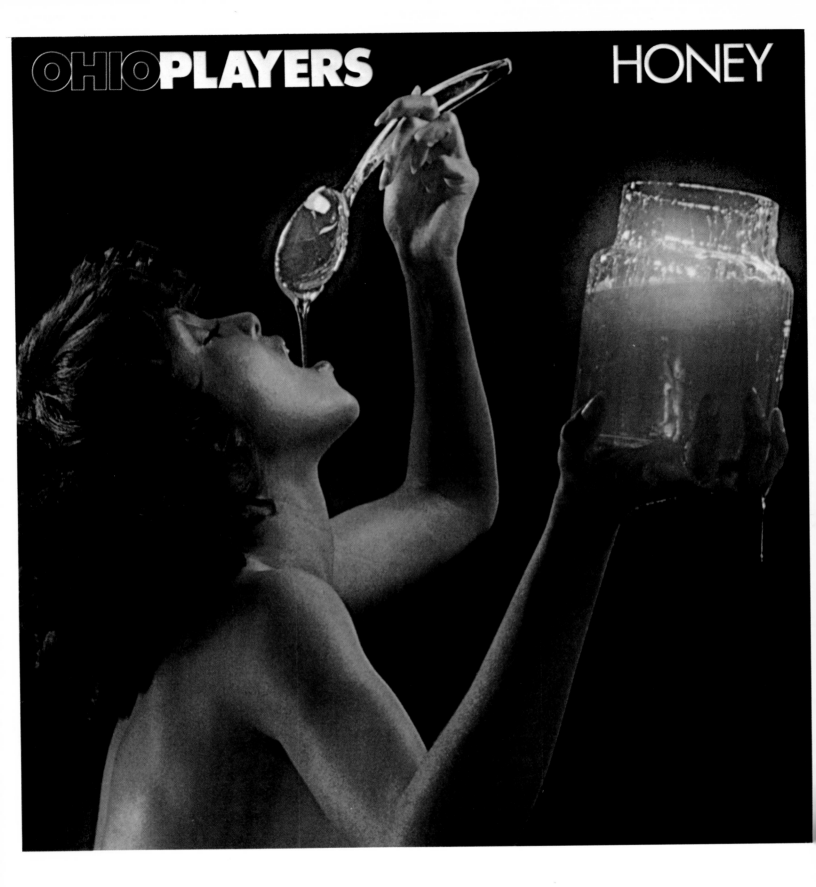

The Ohio Players — Honey
Photography: Richard Fegley
Design: Joe Kotleba/AGI
Art Direction: Jim Ladwig/AGI
Date: 1975 Mercury Records

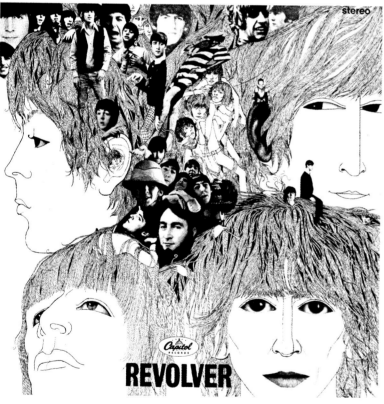

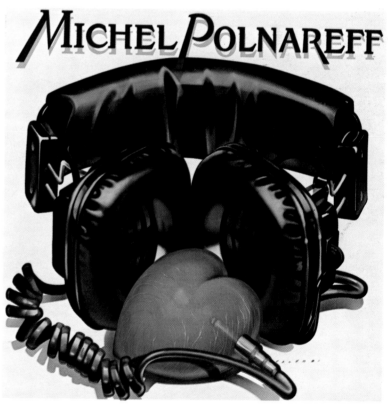

Carly Simon — Playing Possum
Photography and Design: Norman Seeff
Art Direction: Glen Christensen
Date: 1975 Elektra Records

The Rolling Stones — Sticky Fingers
Concept and Photography: Andy Warhol
Design and Graphics: Craigbrauninc.
Date: 1971 Rolling Stones Records

The Beatles — Revolver
Art and Design: Klaus Voorman
Date: 1966 Capitol (EMI) Records

Michel Polnareff
Artist: Peter Palombi
Art Direction: Bob Defrin
Date: 1975 Atlantic Records

Cover paintings by Andy Warhol

90

Paul Anka — The Painter
Artist: Andy Warhol (Courtesy of Mr. Paul Anka)
Art Direction: Ria Lewerke
Date: 1976 United Artists Records

Sky King — Secret Sauce
Artist: Roger Huyssen
Design: Gerard Huerta
Art Direction: John Berg
Date: 1975 Columbia Records

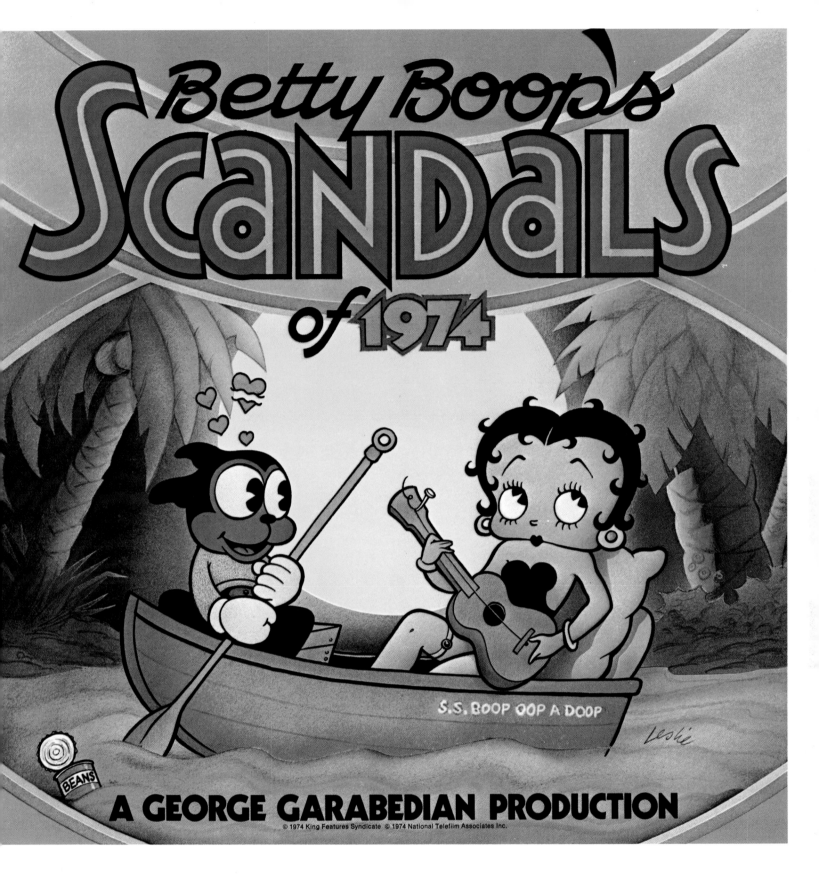

Betty Boop's Scandals of 1974
Artist: Leslie Cabarga
© A George Garabedian Production for Mark 56 Records
Date: 1974 Mark 56 Records

The Mothers of Invention — Weasels Ripped My Flesh
Artist: Neon Park
Art Direction: Ed Thrasher
Date: 1970 Bizarre/Reprise Records

Unpublished Work
Artist: Mick Haggerty/Rod Dyer Inc.
Art Direction: Roland Young
Date: 1971

Claudia Cardinale

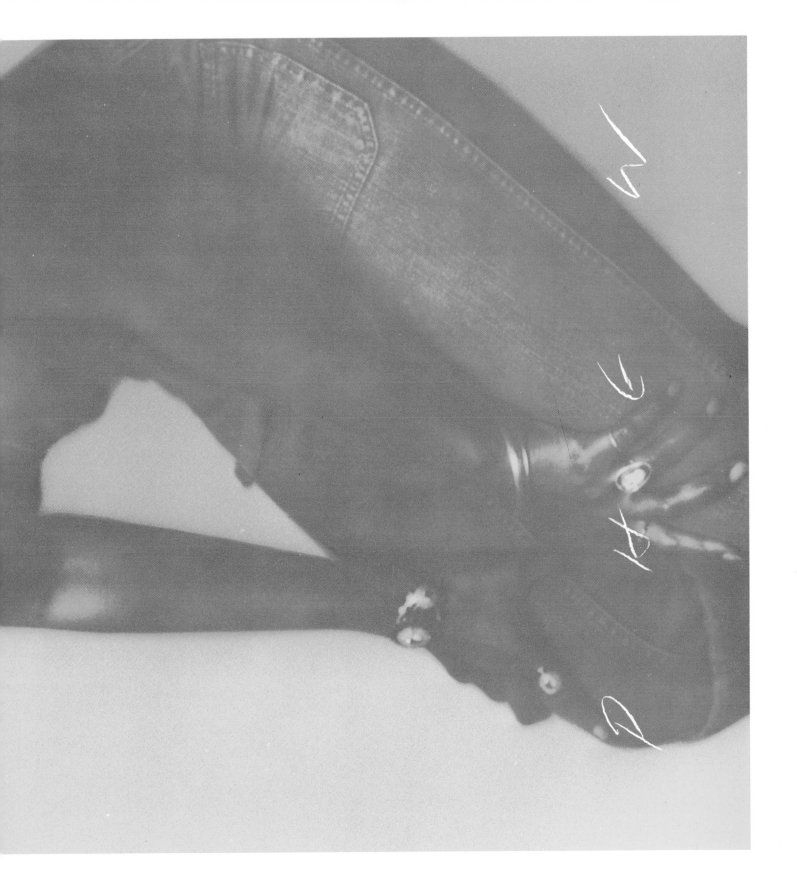

Claudia Lennear — Phew
Art Direction and Design: John Van Hamersveld
Photography: Norman Seeff
Date: 1972 Warner Bros. Records

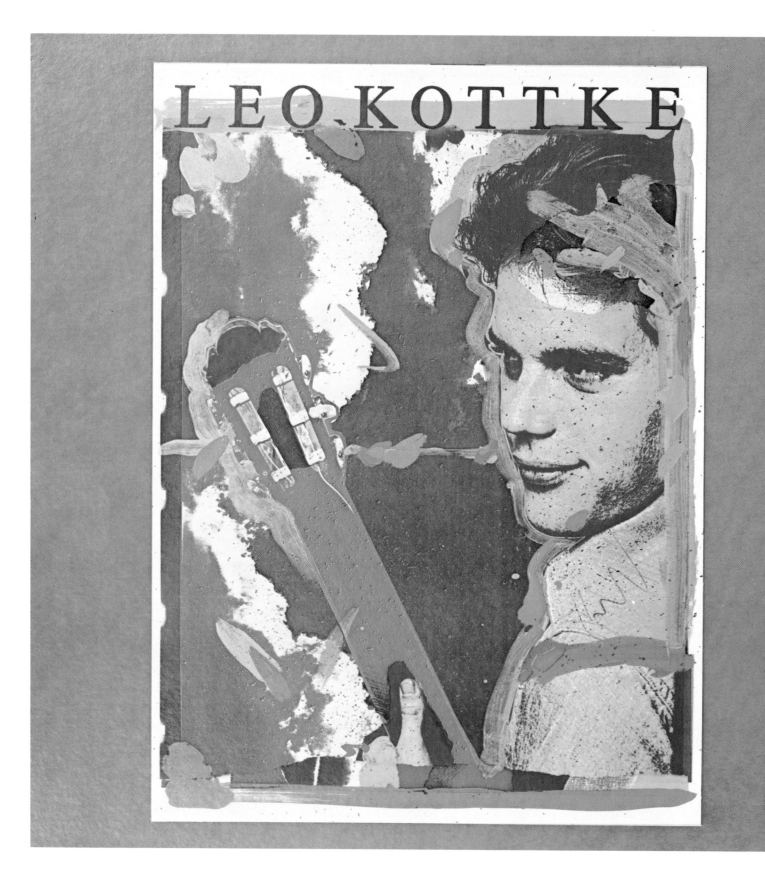

Leo Kottke
Photographic Collage and Design: John Van Hamersveld
Date: 1976 Chrysalis Records

Ferrante and Teicher — Dial M For Music
Artist: Peter Palombi
Art Direction: Mike Salisbury
Date: 1974 United Artists Records

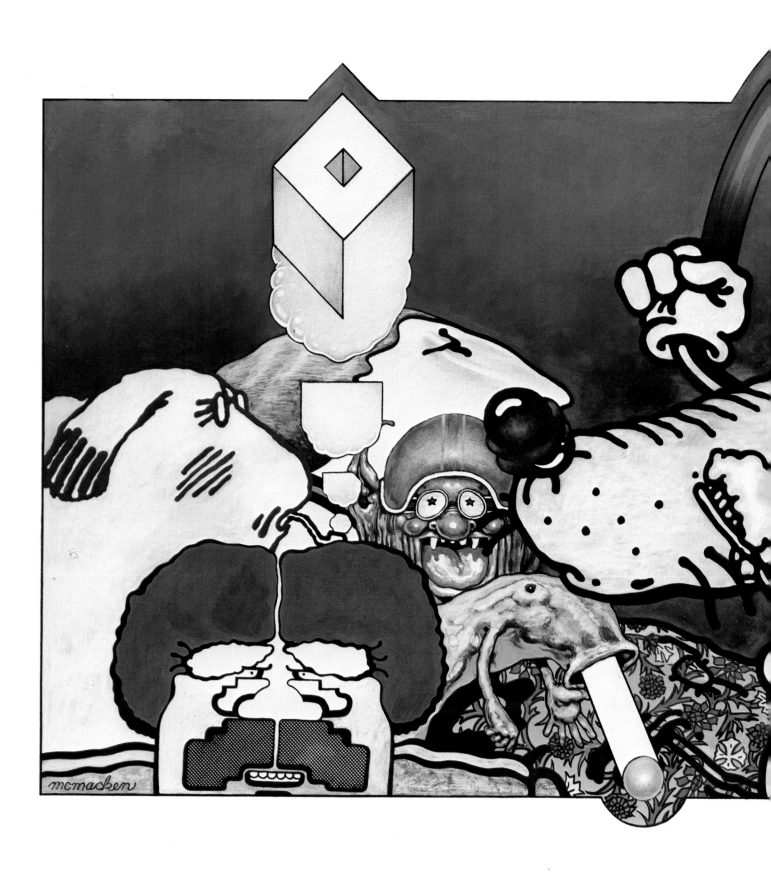

Unpublished Work
Artist: Dave McMacken
Art Direction: Norman Seeff
Date: 1972

Toshiko Akiyoshi/Lew Tabackin Big Band — Tales of a Courtesan
Artist: Stanislaw Fernandes
Art Direction: Dick Smith
Date: 1976 RCA Records

King Harvest
Artist: David Willardson/Star Studios
Concept: Chuck Beeson and Roland Young
Art Direction: Roland Young
Date: 1975 A&M Records

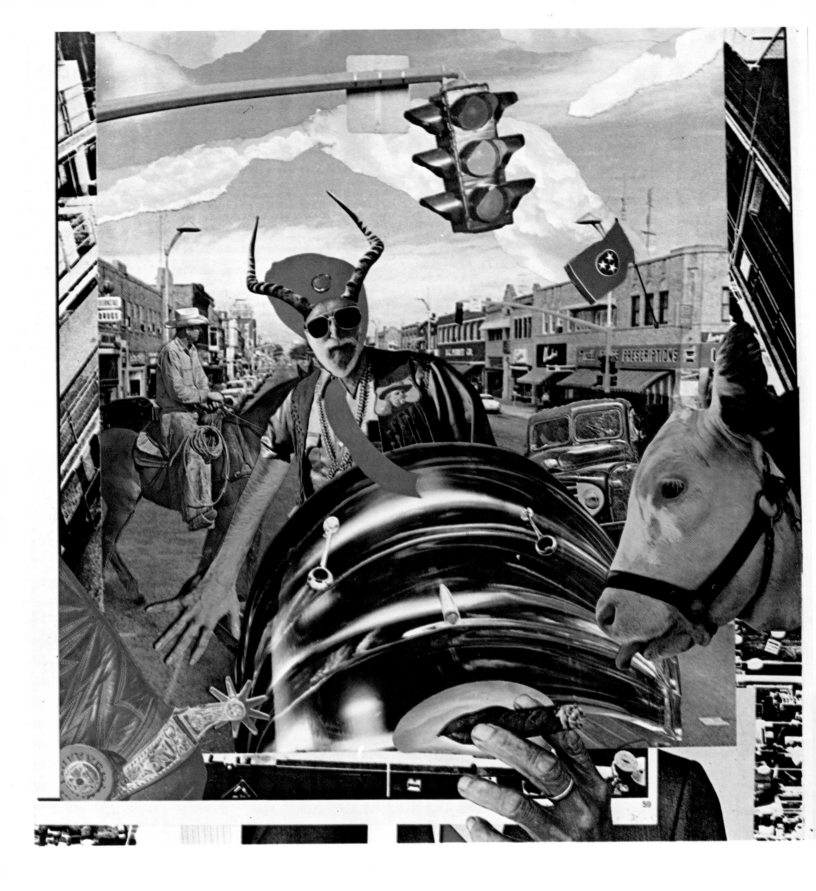

Volunteer Jam
Artist: Lou Beach
Art Direction: Diana Kaylan
Date: 1976 Capricorn Records

The Beckies
Art and Design: Bill Naegels/Rod Dyer Inc.
Art Direction: Toni J. Wadler
Date: 1976 Sire Records

Grateful Dead — Aoxomoxoa
Artist: Rick Griffin
Art Direction: Ed Thrasher
Date: 1969 Warner Bros. Records

Alice Cooper Goes To Hell
Design: Rod Dyer/Brian Hagiwara
Date: 1976 Warner Bros. Records

Bobby Whitlock — Rock Your Sox Off
Art and Design: Mick Haggerty/Art Attack
Art Direction: Diana Kaylan
Date: 1976 Capricorn Records

Russell Morris II
Artist: Dave Jarvis
Cover Design: Tim Bryant/Gribbitt!
Art Direction: Acy Lehman
Date: 1976   RCA Records

Jimmy McGriff — Black Pearl
Artist: John Van Hamersveld
Art Direction: Norman Seèff
Date: 1971 Blue Note Records

Jambalaya — High Rollers
Artist: Mick Haggerty/Rod Dyer, Inc.
Art Direction: Roland Young
Date: 1973 A&M Records

Hummingbird —We Can't Go On Meeting Like This
Photography: John Thornton
Design: John Pasche (Gull Graphics)
Art Direction: Fabio Nicoli
Date: 1977 A&M Records

UFO — Force It
Design and Photography: Hipgnosis
Date: 1975 Chrysalis Records

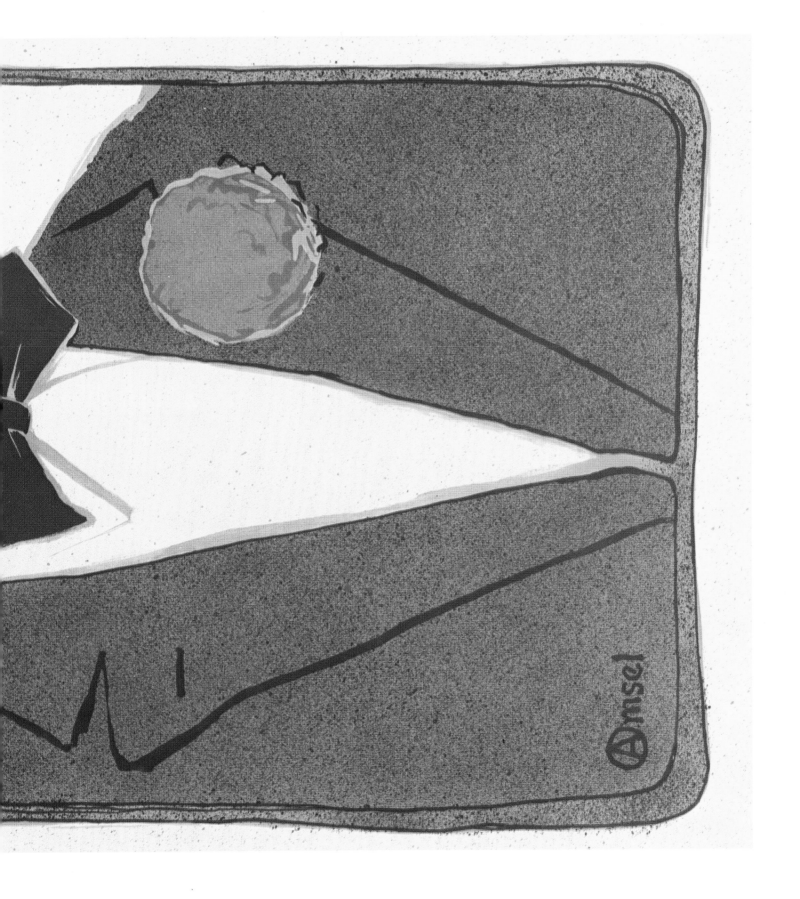

This Is Maurice Chevalier
Artist: Richard Amsel
Art Direction: Joseph Stelmach
Date: 1972 RCA Records

The Rolling Stones — Their Satanic Majesties Request
Photography and Design: Michael Cooper
Cover photo built by The Rolling Stones, Michael Cooper and
Artchie at Pictorial Productions, Mt. Vernon, N.Y.
Date: 1967 London Records

The Beatles — Sgt. Pepper's Lonely Hearts Club Band
Photography: Michael Cooper
Wax Figures: Madame Tussaud's
Concept and Design: MC Productions and The Apple
Staged by Peter Blake and Jann Haworth
Date: 1967 Capitol (EMI) Records

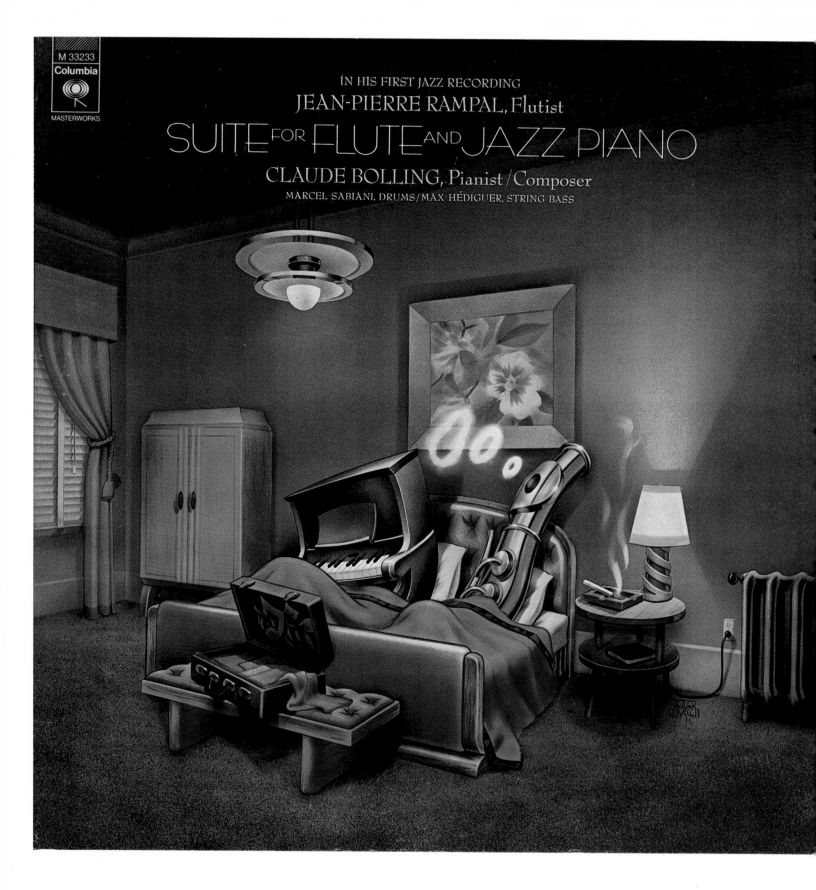

Suite for Flute and Jazz Piano
Artist: Roger Huyssen
Concept and Design: John Berg and Andy Engel
Date: 1975 Columbia Records

Pacific Gas and Electric — Are You Ready
Art and Concept: David Willardson/Star Studios
Logo Design: John Van Hamersveld
Design: Ann Garner
Art Direction: Virginia Team
Date: 1970 Columbia Records

Hustler's Convention
Artist: David Willardson/Star Studios
Art Direction: Ria Lewerke
Date: 1975 United Artists Records

David Bowie — Diamond Dogs
Artist: Guy Peellaert
Art Direction: AGI
Date: 1974 RCA Records

Cactus — Ot 'N Sweaty
Artist: David Willardson/Star Studios
Art Direction: Richard Mantel
Date: 1972 Atco Records

The Kinks — Schoolboys in Disgrace
Artist: Mickey Finn
Art Direction: Pat Doyle
Date: 1975 RCA Records

Trapeze — Hotwire
Artist: Wurlitzer
Art Direction: Seabrook/Graves/Aslett, Assoc.
Date: 1977 Warner Bros. Records

Firesign Theatre — Don't Crush That Dwarf, Hand Me The Pliers
Artist: Robert Grossman
Art Direction: John Berg
Date: 1970 Columbia Records

·BETTE MIDLER·THE DIVINE MISS M·

Bette Midler — The Divine Miss M
Artist: Richard Amsel
Design and Art Direction: Richard Mantel
Date: 1972 Atlantic Records

Radio Dinner
Art, Concept and Design: Charles White III
Date: 1973 National Lampoon

Andy Bey
Artist: Peter Lloyd
Art Direction: Bob Defrin
Date: 1975 Atlantic Records

The Section — Fork It Over
Artist: David Willardson/Star Studios
Art Direction: Roy Kohara
Date: 1977 Capitol Records

The World of Kay Kaiser
Artist: Kim Whitesides
Art Direction: Lester Glassner
Date: 1976 Columbia Records

The Best of Dinah Shore
Artist: Doug Johnson
Art Direction: John Berg and Lester Glassner
Date: 1977 Columbia Records

Richie Havens — The End Of The Beginning
Photography: Moshe Brakha
Design: Junie Osaki
Art Direction: Roland Young
Date: 1976 A&M Records

Capitol Disco Cover
Artist: Taki Ono
Design: Rod Dyer, Inc.
Art Direction: Roy Kohara
Date: 1977 Capitol Records

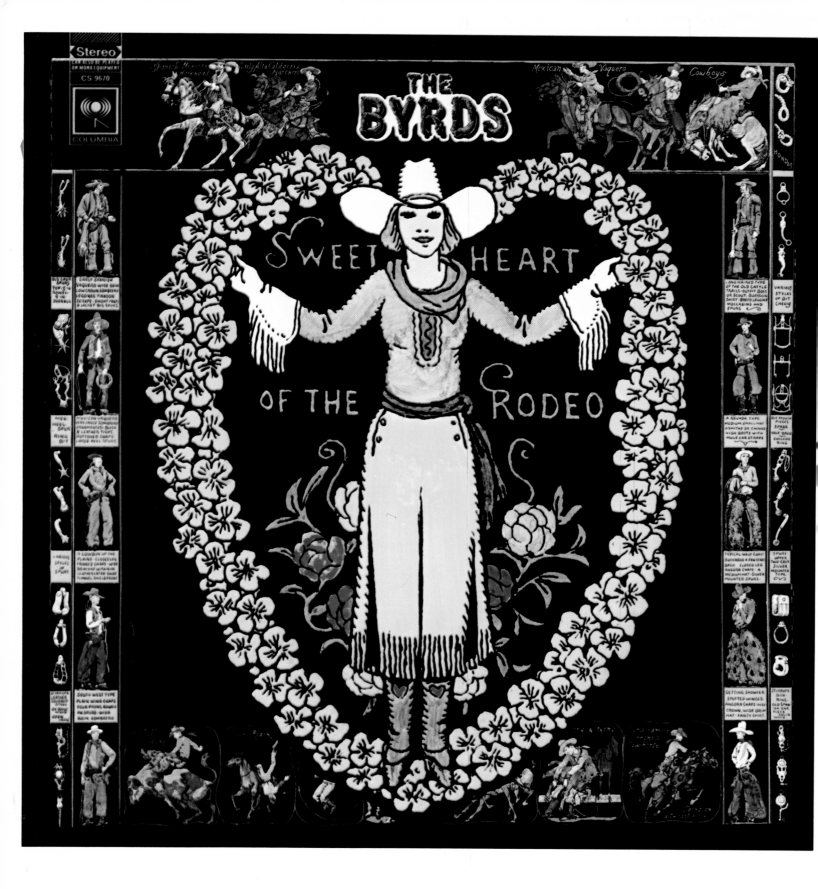

The Byrds — Sweetheart of the Rodeo
Art and Concept: Craig Butler-Snyder/Butler Advertising
Line Drawings: Joe Mora
Art Direction: John Berg
Date: 1970 Columbia Records

Unpublished Work
Artist: Peter Palombi
Art Direction: Ed Thrasher
Date: 1976

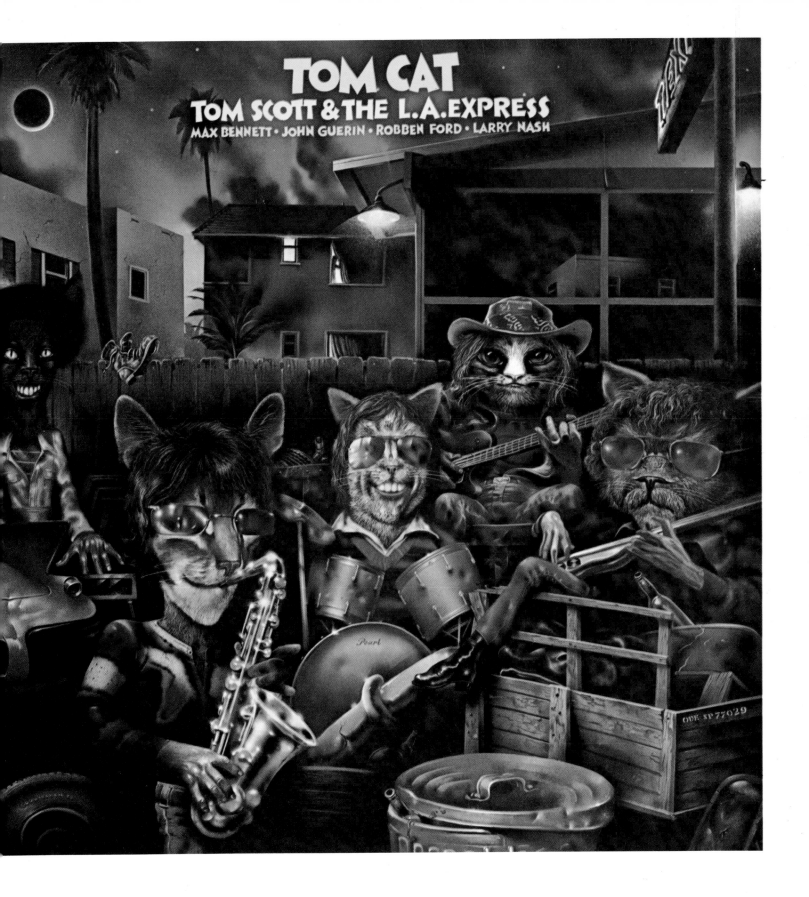

Tom Scott and The L.A. Express — Tom Cat
Artist: Dave McMacken
Art Direction: Chuck Beeson
Date: 1974 Ode Records

The Doors — Strange Days
Photography: Joel Brodsky
Concept and Art Direction: William S. Harvey
Date: 1968 Elektra Records

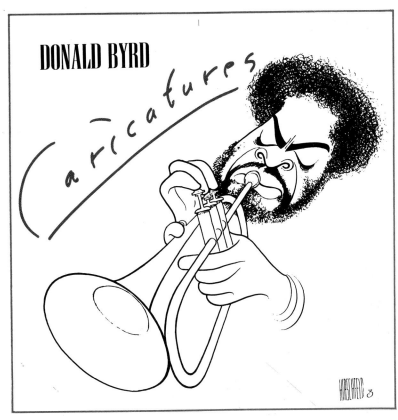

Moonquake
Artist: Phil Carroll
Design and Art Direction: Tony Lane
Date: 1973 Fantasy Records

Donald Byrd — Caricatures
Artist: Hirschfeld
Art Direction: Ria Lewerke
Date: 1976 Blue Note Records

The Rolling Stones — Let It Bleed
Photography: Don McAllester
Concept and Design: Robert Brownjohn
Date: 1969 London Records

MCA-2245

Kalyan
Artist: Uli Boege/Rod Dyer, Inc.
Art Direction: George Osaki
Date: 1977 MCA Records

136

Unpublished Work
Artist: Lou Beach
Date: 1976

We would like to thank all of the following for their kind permission to reprint album covers.

The following are reprinted courtesy of A&M Records, Inc.: First Move, High Rollers, King Harvest, Nils Lofgren, Smokin', The End Of The Beginning, Target, Tom Cat, The Tubes, We Can't Go On Meeting Like This.

The following are reprinted courtesy of ABC Records: Rufus—Featuring Chaka Khan, Steppin', The Beckies

The following are reprinted courtesy of Atlantic Records: Andy Bey, Bad Luck Is All I Have, Blind Faith, Hotline, Is It In?, Larger Than Life, Made In The Shade, Michael Polnareff, Oh Yeah?, Ot 'N Sweaty, Rock 'N Roll Queen, Silk Torpedo, Sticky Fingers, That Is Why You're Overweight, The Divine Miss M, The Don Harrison Band.

The unpublished works on pages 80-81 and 137 appear courtesy of Lou Beach.

The following are reprinted courtesy of Capitol Records: Bang! Music, Book of Dreams, Capitol Disco Cover, Fork It Over.

The following are reprinted courtesy of Capricorn Records, Inc., Macon, Georgia: Rock Your Sox Off; Volunteer Jam; Wipe The Windows, Check the Oil, Dollar Gas.

The following is reprinted courtesy of Chrysalis Records: Force It.

The following are reprinted courtesy of Columbia Records: Are You Ready?; Bitches Brew; Byrdmaniax; Cecilio And Kapano; Cheap Thrills; Chicago X; Dick Powell In Hollywood; Don't Crush That Dwarf, Hand Me The Pliers; Fountains Of Light; Ginseng Woman; Heavy Weather; Kinky Friedman; Lasso From El Paso; Le Sacre Du Printemps; Moving Targets; Peace And Quiet; Salongo; Santana—Greatest Hits; Secret Sauce; Silk Degrees; Slow Dancer; Starcastle; Suite For Flute And Jazz Piano; Super Chief; Supersnazz; Sweathog; The Best Of Dinah Shore; The Sidewalks Of New York; The Sweetheart Of The Rodeo; The World Of Kay Kaiser; Underground.

The following are reprinted courtesy of EMI Records Ltd.: Atom Heart Mother, Revolver, Sgt Pepper's Lonely Hearts Club Band.

The following are reprinted courtesy of Fantasy Records: Moonquake, Starstruck.

Betty Boop's Scandals of 1974 is a George Garabedian Production/Anaheim, California; Betty Boop © 1974 King Features Syndicate.

The following are reprinted courtesy of Island Records, Inc.: No Reservations, The James Montgomery Band.

The following are reprinted courtesy of Kelley/Mouse Studios: Book of Dreams, Europe '72.

The cover art for the following are reproduced by kind permission of London Records, Inc. and Abkco Records: Let It Bleed, Their Satanic Majesties Request.

The following are reprinted courtesy of MCA Records, Inc.: American Graffiti, Kalyan.

The following are reprinted courtesy of Mercury (Phonogram) Records: Fire, Honey, There Must Be More To Love Than This.

Give And Take is reprinted courtesy of Motown Record Corporation.

A Fifth of Beethoven is reprinted courtesy of Private Stock Records, Ltd.

The following are reprinted courtesy of RCA Records: Bark, Diamond Dogs, Dragonfly, Russell Morris II, Schoolboys In Disgrace, Tales Of The Courtesan, This Is Helen O'Connell, This Is Maurice Chevalier.